USING FOUCAULT'S METHODS

INTRODUCING QUALITATIVE METHODS provides a series of volumes which introduce qualitative research to the student and beginning researcher. The approach is interdisciplinary and international. A distinctive feature of these volumes is the helpful student exercises.

One stream of the series provides texts on the key methodologies used in qualitative research. The other stream contains books on qualitative research for different disciplines or occupations. Both streams cover the basic literature in a clear and accessible style, but also cover the 'cutting edge' issues in the area.

SERIES EDITOR
David Silverman (Goldsmiths College)

EDITORIAL BOARD
Michael Bloor (University of Wales, Cardiff)
Barbara Czarniawska-Joerges (University of Gothenburg)
Norman Denzin (University of Illinois, Champagne)
Barry Glassner (University of Southern California)
Jaber Gubrium (University of Florida, Gainesville)
Anne Murcott (South Bank University)
Jonathan Potter (Loughborough University)

TITLES IN THE SERIES
Doing Conversation Analysis: A Practical Guide
Paul ten Have

Using Foucault's Methods
Gavin Kendall and Gary Wickham

USING FOUCAULT'S METHODS

Gavin Kendall
and
Gary Wickham

SAGE Publications
London · Thousand Oaks · New Delhi

First published 1999
Reprinted 2000

SAGE Publications Ltd
6 Bonhill Street
London EC2A 4PU

SAGE Publications Inc
2455 Teller Road
Thousand Oaks, California 91320

SAGE Publications India Pvt Ltd
32, M-Block Market
Greater Kailash – I
New Delhi 110 048

British Library Cataloguing in Publication Data

A catalogue record for this book is
available from the British Library

    ISBN 0 7619 5716 2
    ISBN 0 7619 5717 0 (pbk)

Library of Congress catalog record available

Typeset by Type Study, Scarborough, North Yorkshire
Printed in Great Britain by Biddles Ltd, *www.biddles.co.uk*

Contents

Preface

As is obvious from even a glance at the catalogue of any academic publisher, much recent research has been conducted in the shadow of Foucault. While researchers in this emerging tradition make use of some standard qualitative methods in the social sciences – including textual analysis, observation and historical inquiry – they also introduce into social interpretation an 'extra dimension': a new way of understanding the intersection of power and knowledge.

In this book we set out the various ways in which Foucault's work has been taken up by social analysts to exploit this 'extra dimension' in such a way that postgraduate and undergraduate students can adapt it to their needs.

Our book is organised around two themes:

1 History, archaeology, genealogy and discourse as the cornerstones of Foucault's methods.
2 Science and culture as important objects of analysis for those using Foucault's methods.

The book's five main chapters are organised into two parts in line with these two themes. Chapters 1 and 2 form the first part, setting out Foucault's 'extra dimension' through discussions of his very particular use of each of history, archaeology, genealogy and discourse. Chapters 3, 4 and 5 form the second part, discussing various ways in which Foucault's methods have been used to analyse science (Chapters 3 and 4) and culture (Chapter 5). Chapter 6 is a summary conclusion. Each chapter has exercises built into it to illustrate its main methodological points.

We employ a style which we hope encourages students' passion for Foucault but directs it to the many ways in which Foucault's methods (and those of his 'friends') have been used in the analysis of social order. This involves us adopting the perspective of various quizzical students as they attempt to make sense of the material in terms of their own ambitions as scholars.

Some cautionary remarks are necessary before we begin the book proper. First of all, it may be suggested that there are no such persons as 'Foucaultians' and that there is no such thing as a 'Foucaultian method' (for example, Megill [1985] argues that Foucault's approach was so 'unmethodological' that his only apparently methodological text, *The Archaeology of Knowledge*, was really a spoof). As we discuss in Chapter 1, we have some sympathy with this scepticism, but still believe there is a place for a text which tries to introduce some basic themes in research of this type; the alternative is, perhaps, to suggest that there is something mystical or inexplicable about Foucault's approach. Maybe it's only possible to get across something of the 'spirit' of Foucault's inquiries, but, even if we can only go that far, we think it's worth trying to give as straightforward an introduction as possible.

Second, our book has its origins in a certain disquiet about Foucault's reception in the academic world. Too often he is presented as one of the 'postmoderns', which has meant that many hastily write him off as one of those wild, slightly mad French theorists. To the contrary, we regard Foucault as a most careful investigator. His work is not the product of idle speculation or groundless grand theorising, but emerged from a huge amount of very careful research. It is also the case that Foucault's work does not fit very well into either the camp of 'critical' research – we do not think Marxism or feminism, for example, can be easily added on to Foucault's insights – or the camp of 'liberal' research – by which we mean that Foucault's thoroughgoing scepticism about such notions as 'truth', 'progress' or 'values' means that it is difficult to see his work as building on other work in similar areas. This curious position that Foucault occupies means that while he is frequently name-checked, his approach is rarely taken seriously.

Third, a great deal of the book concerns itself with science studies, especially with the work of Bruno Latour. We are not sure whether Latour would mind being included in a book of Foucaultian methods; while Foucault's name crops up fairly regularly in Latour's early work, it seems to have slowly disappeared from his intellectual horizon (judging by whom he cites, at any rate). We are not dogmatic about this: we see Latour's approach as broadly reconcilable with Foucault's, and it is important for our purposes because it demonstrates a way of doing 'Foucaultian' research which is not necessarily historical.

Acknowledgements

Although we take full responsibility for any solecisms contained within this book, we thank the following for their help with anything that is good about it: James Butterfield, Jo Goodie, Jeremy Kendall, Kate Kendall, Trisha Kendall, Ivan Krisjansen, Jeff Malpas, Mike Michael, Clare O'Farrell, Clifford Shearing, Katherine Sheehan, and especially our encouraging series editor, David Silverman. We also thank the staff at Sage for making working on this book such a pleasant experience.

Part I

HISTORY, ARCHAEOLOGY, GENEALOGY AND DISCOURSE AS THE CORNERSTONES OF FOUCAULT'S METHODS

1

'I'm interested in Foucault, but why should I be interested in history?'

CONTENTS

'Foucault helps us see that sex isn't what nineteenth-century reform fanatics thought it was', Inzammam tells his class-mates during a presentation.

'Reading Madness and Civilization *makes it clear to me that women are constructed as mentally ill by a patriarchal system of health management,' Jenny contributes on her first evening at the 'recent French theory' reading group her friends have been raving about.*

Zeeha, trying to explain to her father why he's wrong to see corporal punishment as a solution to the rising crime rate in their town, tells him she's learned from a book she's just read as part of her Criminology course that punishment is part of a larger system of discipline for societies, not a response to crime.

Inzammam, Jenny and Zeeha are all good students with a new-found passion for Foucault. Let's follow them, at least some of the way, through their student careers to see how their passion for Foucault develops and try to help them over the obstacles which so often pop up in the paths of those who seek to use Foucault.

The first thing to be said is to reassure these three good students that they should not feel embarrassed about bumping into obstacles in seeking to use Foucault's methods. Foucault's methods are not easy to follow. Even though we can sensibly regard *The Archaeology of Knowledge*, 'The

Order of Discourse' and 'Questions of Method' (Foucault 1972, 1981a, 1981b) as methodological in tone, they do not add up to a coherent statement of his methodology and they hardly constitute a user-friendly 'how to' guide to Foucaultian scholarship. Inzammam, Jenny and Zeeha are keeping the company of more experienced scholars in stumbling at some methodological hurdles.

The first trap they have fallen into is to place limits on the use of history involved in Foucaultian scholarship. Helping them avoid this trap is the work of the remainder of this chapter. Inzammam, Jenny and Zeeha are right to see that Foucault uses history as his main technique to make his points about sexuality, madness, punishment, the self, the body, and so forth. However, they are wrong to try to limit this move such that they are free to make *ahistorical* political points about the present and/or the future.

Yes, Foucault does problematise simplistic categorisations of nineteenth-century attitudes to sex, the use of madness as a fixed diagnostic category, and the portrayal of punishment as no more than a component in a means–ends equation. But his problematisations never stop, his histories never stop. Inzammam speaks of sexuality as if we enlightened twentieth-century folk have overcome the hang-ups of our forebears; Jenny and Zeeha speak of madness and punishment respectively as if some 'progress' has been or might be made, or conversely as if modern life is 'worse' than the past.

The Foucaultian method's use of history is not a turn to teleology, that is, it does not involve assumptions of progress (or regress). This is why we say it involves histories that never stop: they cannot be said to stop because they cannot be said to be going anywhere. To use history in the Foucaultian manner is to use it to help us see that the present is just as strange as the past, not to help us see that a sensible or desirable present has emerged (Inzammam's error) or might emerge (Jenny's and Zeeha's error). Sometimes the Foucaultian approach to history is referred to as 'history of the present'. Hopefully our discussion here helps make this term clear: Foucaultian histories are histories of the present not because understanding an ideal or complete present is the spur to investigation (this is sometimes called 'whig history'). Foucaultians are not seeking to find out how the present has emerged from the past. Rather, the point is to use history as a way of *diagnosing* the present (on this point, see Rose 1990).

When we use history, if we are to gain the maximum benefit from the Foucaultian method, we must ensure that we do not allow this history to stop, do not allow it to settle on a patch of imagined sensibleness in the field of strangeness; as Foucault himself says, albeit in a different context, we should seek 'to use it, to deform it, to make it groan and protest' (1980a: 54). History should be used not to make ourselves comfortable, but rather to disturb the taken-for-granted. Inzammam should be aware that late twentieth-century attitudes to sex are as much part of the complex of power and knowledge around the idea of sexuality as were nineteenth-century attitudes. Jenny and Zeeha should be aware that feminist objections to current psychiatric arrangements and liberal objections to certain regimes of punishment are caught up with the complexes of power and knowledge around madness and punishment as much as are the arrangements and regime they would like to see changed.

We suggest two effective techniques to keep oneself aware of this pitfall:

1   Look for contingencies instead of causes.
2   Be as sceptical as possible in regard to all political arguments.

Look for contingencies instead of causes

Looking for contingencies instead of causes is not quite as difficult as it might sound. Imagine yourself at the centre of a site of one of your investigations – let's take punishment as an example. First, imagine yourself as an administrator of a new prison in 1870. You attempt to carry out instructions from central government to the effect that prisoners are to be treated humanely but, in line with new penological thinking, not encouraged to speak to one another. You have to balance this demand with the difficulty of disciplining the prison's guards, who are used to more direct methods, often violent but nonetheless based on regular interaction between prisoners. As well, you feel hamstrung by the fact that other administrators at the prison have not received the same classics-based university education that you have received, but have secured their positions by means of family connections; they see no logic in the government's directive and side readily with the guards in the 'tried and true' way of going about things.

Now, quickly transport yourself to the twelfth century. You are the dispenser of justice in a blood-feud system. One man has stolen a pig from another. The system of justice in which you are a major player is restitutive rather than punitive. This means that when a person is wronged the wrong-doer must restore something to the person wronged; punishment is not a direct consideration. In line with common practice you are present to oversee the pig owner taking the arm of the pig stealer, for this is considered proper restitution. Things go somewhat awry when the pig owner, feeling particularly aggrieved because it was his best pig and not just any old pig, tries to take an eye as well as the agreed arm. In other words, he feels the need to punish, not just to restore. You have to respond.

We will offer another example later in this chapter, as part of Exercise 1.1.

Both these imaginary situations contains more contingencies than you can poke a stick at; that is, they are littered with developments sensibly seen as *accidents of history*. When we describe an historical event as contingent, what we mean is that the emergence of that event was not necessary, but was one possible result of a whole series of complex relations between other events. It takes far more intellectual effort to see these developments in terms of causes and effects than it does to accept them as contingencies. This is why we say the technique of looking for contingencies instead of causes is not as difficult as it sounds. The problem is, most of us get into the habit of looking for causes. We need to break this habit in favour of the easier move of accepting them as contingencies.

In the first example the idea of imprisonment as a punishment is a contingency. The position of administrator as a separate career position is a contingency – while such positions were common enough in Ancient Greece and Rome, they disappeared as a common feature of European life for quite some time, returning only in the wake of other contingencies like the development of printing and of large-scale government budgets based on new taxation methods. So, the idea of a central government powerful enough to issue instructions about various matters and have them treated with any degree of seriousness away from the direct influence of the immediate personnel of that government is itself also a contingency. Still another is the idea of treating prisoners humanely yet not allowing them regular speaking contact with one another, which seems to our late twentieth-century way of thinking a contradiction – it is a contingency of the development of penological knowledge, itself a contingency as well. It is also a contingency that the prison's guards are more comfortable with more direct methods of controlling prisoners. It is a contingency that some administrators receive a university education while others do not. It is a contingency that classics was the discipline base of an administrator's university education in the nineteenth century; today it is much more likely to be economics or some other social science. It is a contingency that family connections were a more common route to government jobs in nineteenth-century Europe than they are today, or than they were then in, say, China, where a long tradition of public examinations had dominated as a means of deciding such matters. It is a contingency that governmental logic is more widespread at some times than at others.

Now, when we say that these events are contingent, this is not the same thing as saying that anything could have happened or did happen. Of course, there were definite pressures at work which meant that punishment started to become 'humane', for example. The point that Foucault regularly makes, however, is that so often our much-cherished advances are the quite accidental result of some apparently unrelated change. Of course Foucault is not the only social theorist who has made this point. Max Weber, for example, spoke of the 'unintended consequences' of history; for example, how certain puritan theological concerns could lead to some rather surprising turns – like the inventions of tarmac or chocolate.

Our group of budding Foucaultian scholars should not despair at this jumble of contingencies from just one small example. As we suggested, seeing contingencies instead of causes is a habit that is easy to acquire. It is more a question of *not* taking the steps to introduce causes into the equation than it is of doing something extra. To draw up a list of contingencies such as that presented above certainly involves historical investigation – a knowledge of some facts, to put it bluntly – but it does not require an exercise in artificially designating some items on the list to be primary and others secondary, or even tertiary, or designating those on the list to be in some subordinate relation to an item not on the list but which one is supposed to know as the primary source for details which make up such lists. To the Foucaultian way of thinking, such exercises in causal logic are futile. For Foucaultians, there is no reason to suppose, in considering this small historical example, that the training of prison administrators is in a relation of subordination to the dominance of classics as a discipline base, or the other way around, or that the distribution of positions based on family connections is in a relation of subordination to the development of governmental logic, or the other way around, and so on. And certainly the Foucaultian way of approaching history can have no truck with the idea that any one of the contingencies listed, say the imperative to keep prisoners from speaking to one another, is in a relation of subordination to the unspoken, unseen development of capitalism and its need for a quiescent workforce.

It might help you to learn this technique if, each time you deal with an historical example, you make use of a device sometimes employed by historians – the diagram with arrows. Of course you will have to completely invert its standard format to have it help you learn Foucaultian modes of scholarship, but this could well be a boost to its educative value: where the historians concerned draw the arrows in the diagram to demonstrate causal flows from subordinate to superordinate components, by always making the arrows double-ended and by drawing them such that they connect every component to every other component, and/or by leaving the arrows out of the diagram altogether, you will actually demonstrate the absence of causal flows, you will show how components have only contingent relations with one another, that, to put it bluntly, they may be connected in any pattern or they may not be connected at all.

It almost goes without saying that this will leave your diagram looking either bare and bereft of pattern or order, or alternatively looking like a mass of jumbled lines, again with no pattern or order. Now you're starting to catch on. A couple of French scholars quite close to Foucault – Gilles Deleuze and Félix Guattari – suggested in a famous essay (1988) that patterns of knowledge should be seen as analogous not to a tree with its unidirectional pattern of growth from roots up to branches and leaves via a solid trunk, but to a rhizome – a collection of root-like tentacles with no pattern to their growth, a set of tentacles which grow in unpredictable ways, even growing back into each other. You may find this contrast of analogies helpful in thinking through this aspect of Foucault's methods.

Let's work quickly through the second of the examples we constructed above together and we can then leave you to handle the third example on your own as the first exercise of this chapter.

The very idea of a blood-feud system of justice is the first contingency you bump into in this example. Straight away the skills of contingency spotting you are fast acquiring will be tested to the limit, for it is all too easy in a case like this one to assume that the intervening eight hundred years have been filled with that mysterious substance called progress and that the system of justice which prevails in your modern setting is vastly superior to that featured in this example. Foucaultian contingency spotting will soon teach you simply to see a blood-feud system as one system and the modern system you're used to as another and teach you to leave it at that. In this spirit you will recognise restitutive justice as another contingency and accept as part of this that when a person is wronged the wrong-doer must restore something to the person wronged without consideration of punishment. This step will not prove too difficult if you bear in mind the modern distinction between criminal and civil law. Remember that once O.J. Simpson was found innocent of murder and hence relieved of the danger of punishment, he still had to face a civil trial in which the outcome concerned whether he had to restore something to the immediate families of the murder victims, and if so, how much. This is a legacy of the restitutive systems of justice which only moments ago may have seemed so alien to you.

It is a contingency that the system of justice in question equates loss of an arm with loss of a pig. Again you must guard against false progressivism. Certainly it seems strange to us that body parts should be equated with the loss of livelihood-producing animals, but it helps to realise that it would almost certainly seem strange to the participants in this example that our system sometimes involves the equation of something as abstract as sums of money and confinement with the loss of the lives of loved ones. Recognising strangeness in all social arrangements is an important part of using Foucault's methods.

As well, we should identify contingencies: in the attempt to occasion revenge and punish beyond the prevailing justice arrangements (don't make the mistake of thinking that this is a universal, eternal reaction to such a situation – it happens at some times and in some circumstances and we must treat it as such; this of course is at the heart of the meaning of the term 'contingency'); in the choice of an eye as the 'organ of punishment' (different cultures have placed different value on the eyes as objects of punishment, restitution and revenge – at some times and in some places they have been targets for all three, others for none, and still others for, say, just revenge but not punishment or restitution); and in the role of some sort of neutral moderator, the role you're playing in this example (in some restitutive systems of justice such a figure was involved, but in others the parties sorted things out themselves).

Of course in this example too we must see every contingency in a contingent relationship with every other contingency. There is no necessary pattern to their relating. Indeed there is nothing necessary about their relating at all – they may or may not relate in any way, and if they do, the form of their relationships to one another is not dictated by any pattern or any outside force; to attribute the status of cause and/or effect to any one of them or to any outside force would be to falsely impose some necessity of relating onto them. Again, the drawing of a multi-directional (or anti-directional) arrowed diagram of all the identified contingencies might be helpful.

Okay, now it's your turn.

EXERCISE 1.1

Consider the following example and compile a list of at least four contingencies contained within it. Make some notes on the necessary relations that can sometimes be assumed between your contingencies:

Take yourself forward again, this time right up to the present. You are a schoolteacher faced with a particularly unruly group of pupils. You design and implement a system of graded punishments in an attempt to impose order. You believe you are being very careful as you go about this exercise, drawing on the detailed knowledge of children's development you learned during your training as a teacher. However, a group of parents complains to the school principal that the step in your system which entails keeping miscreant children after school is draconian. You suddenly find yourself disciplined by the principal as, unbeknown to you, the government education authorities, acting in response to a United Nations document about the rights of children, have very recently instructed principals to ban detentions as a cruel and unusual punishment.

To complete the exercise, draw two diagrams, one using two-ended arrows to show every contingency related to every other (just a patternless jumble of related contingencies), and the second, free of arrows, to show no relationship between them (just a patternless jumble of unrelated contingencies). Think about how different this is to an exercise in the application of causal logic.

Be as sceptical as possible in regard to all political arguments

Now let's move on to our other recommended technique – be as sceptical as possible in regard to all political arguments. This technique is closely related to the technique of seeing contingencies instead of causes. It is particularly useful in helping guard against the obstacle we saw Jenny and Zeeha run into – using history to see potential for progress in the future even if it has supposedly not been achieved in the present.

To be sceptical is not to be cynical. Scepticism is a careful, deliberate way of thinking usually traced back to the ancient Greeks. This is not the place for a detailed exposition of the history and practice of different forms of scepticism, though a brief outline will be helpful. Of necessity the outline is very crude (we thank James Butterfield and Jeff Malpas for their help with this sketch; its crudeness stems from the restrictions of our usage, not from their understanding; you might also like to consult Hankinson 1995).

Greek scepticism developed into two distinct camps. One is known loosely as Academic scepticism (after the famous Academy), the other as Pyrrhonian scepticism (after its founder, Pyrrho of Elis, a third-century BC philosopher). Academic scepticism is built around the proposition that we cannot know anything. This proposition is taken as the basis for radical rejection of all truth claims. Pyrrhonistic scepticism is based on the proposition that we cannot know anything, *including the fact that we cannot know anything*. The extra dimension has enormous consequences and allows the Pyrrhonistic proposition to serve as the basis for a decidedly less radical suspension of judgement. It is this second, Pyrrhonian, scepticism that we are urging here.

Pyrrho did not leave any written works, consistent with his complete scepticism. What we know of him comes to us through remaining fragments about him and some of his leading pupils. One such fragment reads:

> Pyrrho's pupil, Timon, says that anyone who is going to lead a happy life must take account of the following three things: first, what objects are like by nature; secondly, what our attitude toward them should be; finally, what will result from those who take this attitude. Now he says that Pyrrho shows that objects are equally indifferent and unfathomable and indeterminable because neither our senses or our judgements are true or false; so for that reason we should not trust in them but should be without judgement and without inclination and unmoved, saying about each thing that it is no more is than is not or both is and is not or neither is or is not. And Timon says that for those who take this attitude the result will first be non-assertion, then tranquillity. (cited in Annas and Barnes 1994: x)

You can see from this that Pyrrhonism, fully developed, is more than a methodological device; it is something approaching a way of life. Don't be alarmed by this as it's true of most philosophical positions when pushed to their limits. We could not hope easily to learn its intricacies as a way of life. What we can and should do is explore the possibilities of the step loosely summarised by the term 'suspension of judgement'. To do this, as we have already suggested, we need not follow Pyrrhonism through all the historical details of its various twists and turns – suffice to say that it had a big revival in the second century AD at the hands of Sextus Empiricus, went into something of a decline, then was revived again from the fifteenth century, eventually gaining a strong foothold in modern thought via thinkers like Montaigne and Hume – but as Sextus provides the most detailed surviving account of what it involves, we should spend a little time with him.

In a book usefully entitled (for our purposes at least) *Outlines of Scepticism* (1994), Sextus suggests that the Pyrrhonistic method involves a rejection of any discovery of truth (the dogmatists' position) and of any total denial of the possibility of discovery of truth (the Academics' position) in favour of indefinite continuation of investigations. This aspect of Pyrrhonian scepticism – one of two main aspects – Sextus calls 'investigative'. Crucially, for us, it entails careful description of appearances:

> By way of a preface let us say that on none of the matters to be discussed do we affirm that things are just as we say they are: rather, we report descriptively on each item according to how it appears to us at the time. (Sextus Empiricus 1994: 3)

The other main aspect of Pyrrhonism for Sextus is 'suspensive'; this is the suspension of judgement highlighted above. Sextus says the best way to move toward this goal is to 'set out oppositions'. This means constantly dividing each of appearances and thoughts – the sum total of knowledge for the Pyrrhonian sceptic – into two: one and its opposite; that is, a thought and its opposite, an appearance and its opposite. The idea is not to affirm or deny any proposition, but to move away from the possibility of doing so and toward the desired suspension of judgement. By continually seeing only oppositions – 'to every account an equal account is opposed' (Sextus Empiricus 1994: 5–6) – the mind will, it is claimed, eventually stop judging. This procedure, again, is much easier said than done, but it is extremely valuable.

It should be clear that appearances are important for the Pyrrhonian sceptic. Unwilled, passive appearances, according to Sextus, are the only bases on which a Pyrrhonian sceptic can properly assent to a proposition. But – be careful here – this is a very limited form of assent: confronted with the proposition that honey is sweet, the Pyrrhonian sceptic will assent that honey appears sweet, but will not be drawn on the question of whether it really is or is not sweet; this is a matter for perpetual investigation and hence for suspension of judgement. Sextus tells us that Pyrrhonian sceptics accept appearances as the guidance of human nature because they accept the appearance that humans are naturally capable of perception and thought (hence the statement above that appearances and thoughts are the sum total of knowledge). In line with this, they accept the necessity of feelings such as hunger, cold, heat and thirst, they accept the operation of whatever customs and laws appear to be operating, and they accept the operation of whatever expert knowledge appears to be operating (such as medicine) (Sextus Empiricus 1994: 8–9).

Sextus also takes us through a series of complex steps in elaborating the idea of oppositions – the opposition of what appears to what appears, of what is thought to what is thought, of what appears to what is thought (and vice versa), what is present to what is past or future (and vice versa), even what is present to what is present. We need not follow him completely down this path – it is further than we need to go for our purposes

– but one of his summary statements is worth quoting as a means to conclude our dealings with him (note how it takes us towards suspension of judgement):

> Before the founder of the school to which you adhere was born, the argument of the school, which is no doubt sound, was not yet apparent, although it was [in the eyes of the present] really there in nature. In the same way, it is possible that the argument opposing the one you have just propounded is really there in nature but not yet apparent to us; so we should not yet assent to what is now thought to be a powerful argument. (Sextus Empiricus 1994: 12)

What is most important for us at this juncture – and, we suggest, for folk such as Inzammam, Jenny and Zeeha – is to devise the most straightforward way to suspend judgement such as to gain maximum benefit from the Foucaultian approach to the historical study of various objects, but before we do let's briefly consider one published work which makes at least some use of a Pyrrhonian approach in using Foucault's methods.

As one of a group of texts which have sought to use Foucault's methods to outline the conditions under which certain modern educational techniques have emerged, allowing us the possibility of viewing education in a new way, Ian Hunter's (1989) account of the invention of the aesthetic citizen allows us to understand the realm of personal experience as one which is neither fundamentally individualistic nor one which results from the imposition of a dominant ideology. Hunter is able to demolish the arguments of those for whom education is either class control or a victory for enlightenment thinking; he is able to do this precisely because he uses history without judgements.

The nineteenth-century educational reforms of David Stow are crucial for Hunter, and it is through his analysis of Stow's contribution that Hunter points out where most theorists of education go wrong:

> [They] assume that education is a manifestation of culture, pictured as the historical reconciliation of an exemplary opposition between the self-realising and the utilitarian, the self-expressive and the normative. They disagree only over whether this universal movement towards the complete development of human capacities has already occurred or has been blocked by a freezing of the dialectic on the side of 'class cultural control'. However, it seems to be the case that self-realisation and social norms, self-discovery and moral training, are by no means opposed to each other in Stow's modified version of the pedagogical disciplines. Quite the opposite: it was in the supervised freedom of the playground that moral norms would be realised through self-expressive techniques; and it was in this space that the forms of self-discovery organised around the individual would *permit* the realisation of new social norms at the level of the population. (Hunter 1988: 38–9, emphasis in original)

Hunter's counter-intuitive conclusion arises precisely because, in taking Foucault seriously, he refuses history as the search for ahistorical political judgements. He refuses to make judgements about causality (he is especially adept at refusing those causal stories which are so familiar that they are usually unquestioned). He stresses the unintended consequences of action. You should be able to see that Hunter does not make assumptions about the relation between the present and the past: he does not think the past inferior (because unenlightened – usually the liberal error) or superior (because naive – usually the Marxist error).

In returning to Inzammam, Jenny and Zeeha, we stress that in one sense the suspension of judgement is at the heart of all modern intellectual inquiry, not only that line of inquiry just discussed. When we investigate, say, religions, work practices, family relationships, or any other object of intellectual inquiry, we are of course supposed to keep our personal judgements out of the picture. Inzammam, Jenny, Zeeha and every other student who has done or is doing a course in the humanities, social sciences or even hard sciences anywhere in the western world knows this already. The suspension of judgement we are talking about here is, it should be clear from the above discussion of Hunter's work, of a different order. It is neither of the simple 'keep your judgements out of your work' variety (which we can expect of students anyway), nor that of the sophisticated full-on practitioner of Pyrrhonism (which, as we said, is far too much to expect), but something in between.

Suspending second-order judgements

The suspension of judgement involved in good Foucaultian use of history is largely about suspending judgements other than those you happen to recognise as your own: what we call second-order judgements. From the outset we stress that with even this intermediate form of the suspension of judgement no one ever totally succeeds in this objective (at least no-one who remains active in intellectual inquiry). To escape from second-order judgements completely would be to go all the way down the path of the Pyrrhonian way of life – something which we keep saying is well beyond the scope of a training in Foucaultian methods (to give you some idea, it would equate to achieving the mental and physical discipline necessary to become a Zen Buddhist monk; indeed, given that Pyrrho was known to have travelled with Alexander the Great through what is now India, there is a least a shred of evidence that the two may be related). It is the *process* of attempting to escape the grip of second-order judgements which is central to Foucaultian historical methods, not so much the outcome of each attempt. The process must involve a genuine *attempt*, but not necessarily complete success (on the inevitability of failure in intellectual and governmental projects, see Malpas and Wickham 1995, 1997).

So, what exactly are the targets of this methodological technique? When any aspect of any object being investigated is granted a status (perhaps this status is labelled 'cause', perhaps something else) which draws its authority from another investigation, a second-order judgement is made: a judgement made previously is exercised, brought out from its kennel and given a walk. In this way, you make judgements without them being technically your own judgements. This is the second-order level of judgement the Foucaultian technique aims to suspend; it is second-order judgements which allow ahistorical political points into the picture. Another cluster of examples, based on each of Inzammam's, Jenny's and Zeeha's reading of a particular text by Foucault, will help make this clearer.

Remember that we are trying to help our group of students avoid the trap of setting limits on the historicisation involved in Foucaultian scholarship. More particularly we are trying to help them avoid making *ahistorical* political points about the present and/or the future.

In one of his later books, *The Care of the Self* (1986), Foucault builds a careful picture of techniques developed by the ancient Romans for establishing regimes of self-management, including dream analysis and the analysis of marital behaviours. For us, this is Foucault at his best. It is hard to find a second-order judgement in this volume; it is free of ahistorical political claims based on such judgements. Foucault suspends such judgements to the point where we are presented with a simple and elegant historical compilation of self-management techniques. Many students (and some others) find this a frightening prospect. So used are they to the presence of second-order judgements in historical investigations of such social objects – the basis of their ahistorical political claims – that when confronted with a text which has suspended them, they are forced to invent them. Such an error often takes the following form: while Foucault's history is accepted at face value on first reading, the process does not stop there; at least one more reading is performed, usually by force of habit rather than conscious design, and it is through this and subsequent readings that second-order judgements creep in and ahistorical political claims are made.

Inzammam, Jenny and Zeeha have each developed their Foucaultian interests to the point where they have read *The Care of the Self*. Inzammam has read it for an advanced class he is taking in social theory; Jenny has read it as the next text in a line of Foucault's books her flourishing reading group is working its way through; and Zeeha has read it as background reading for her Criminology studies, trying to ascertain whether some common sense of self informs Roman methods of punishment. We stress again that these three students are good students, working well in their student careers and learning to be good Foucaultian scholars; we highlight their errors because they are common errors, not because these students are particularly error-prone.

Inzammam accepts Foucault's history at face value on his first reading and then habitually performs another reading. This technique has stood him in good stead in his advanced theory class; he has made good grades for seeing connections between Weber's *Protestant Ethic and the Spirit of Capitalism*, Durkheim's *Elementary Forms of the Religious Life* and Marx's *Eighteenth Brumaire of Louis Bonaparte* in terms of the treatment of outcast groups. In *The Care of the Self* Inzammam's second reading identifies a variety of outcast groups in ancient Rome and proposes an argument that variations occurred between the techniques of self-management available to these groups and more dominant groups. This argument is encouraged in Inzammam's class. Inzammam is able to push the argument further by imposing on ancient Rome some political standards of the late twentieth-century western world. This subsequent reading of Foucault's text sees Inzammam making the point that the non-dominant Roman groups would have benefited from the counselling provisions of certain twentieth-century anti-discrimination legislation.

In discussing Inzammam's error we are not disputing the truth of his ahistorical political claim: whether it is true or false is beside the point. The point is that such claims are not the stuff of good Foucaultian scholarship and our objective here is to show how this error can be avoided. We are not saying that students should not make political claims – this is of course a normal and, unless one attains the status of Pyrrhonian 'monk', an inevitable part of intellectual life; as Bernard Williams puts it, we 'need a politics, in the sense of a coherent set of opinions about the ways in which power should be exercised in modern societies, with what limitations and to what end' (1993: 10–11). What we are saying is that it is possible and desirable to separate such claims from productive readings of Foucault's histories, to put them into a separate category of intellectual existence and use Foucault's methods without habitually exercising this category of existence. The way to do this is, first, to identify the moment when the second-order judgements raise their heads. If we can do this successfully, the second step of isolating ahistorical political claims will be easy.

As we have made clear, the moment of the first appearance of second-order judgements is not the moment when direct political claims are made – not when Inzammam sees a connection with anti-discrimination politics. This is a later stage. Second-order judgements tend to sneak in hiding under the cloak of a mysterious figure being brought to bear on the object being analysed. This 'mysterious figure' is usually a representative of the reading habit pointed to above, perhaps best identified by the name of a particular author, though this can be somewhat misleading. We suggest that the 'mysterious figure' who imports second-order judgements into Inzammam's account is Karl Marx. We suggest further that Marx is the culprit for much second-order judging in the second half of the twentieth century. Before we elaborate this point using Inzammam's error as an example, we should briefly defend Marx by way of cashing out our remark that identifying the source(s) of second-order judgements by the use of the name(s) of particular author(s) is somewhat misleading.

Marx is a convenient resting point for our argument as he does indeed litter his works with methodological encouragement that his readers see politics in everything they read and, of course, he is not at all bashful about making political claims himself. But he can hardly be said to have invented this habit. We might at this point turn our attention to Rousseau and his zeal for making intellectual work a tool of the Revolution as if this were all it could ever be, but this too would be misleading. We suggest we can safely leave the matter by pointing to the existence of ancient debates about the necessity or otherwise of political involvement for living a 'decent' life. Let's just say that as well as being beyond the scope of this book, these debates are still unresolved (it would be remiss of us, however, not to make clear, if it needs clarification, that the Pyrrhonian sceptical position does not regard political involvement as necessary for a decent life; it does not oppose such involvement, it simply accepts the appearance that some people are politically involved). Names like 'Rousseau' and 'Marx' are simply markers – albeit important ones – of contributions to this debate.

The technique which has stood Inzammam in such good stead in his advanced theory class is one dominated by Marx (with the above qualifications, of course). The good grades earned for seeing connections between Weber's, Durkheim's and Marx's texts in terms of the treatment of outcast groups were actually earned, unbeknown to Inzammam, by giving Marx's habits priority over those of the other two. This is not to say that Weber's and Durkheim's texts are free of second-order judgements, only that the habit is much stronger in Marx. Inzammam has learned this habit as good scholarship and Marx is the obvious author used when learning it. 'Always look beneath the surface,' Inzammam has taught himself, with plenty of prompting from his teachers. 'I can find political connections if I look hard enough.' This is certainly true, but it is also – crucially, we say – a judgement Inzammam is importing into his reading.

The judgement, note carefully, is that there is something there, something hidden, not so much that the something is political. That it is something political is the next step, followed, in Inzammam's case, by a step that identifies it as something to do with outcast groups (and then by another step which identifies it as something with a possible connection to anti-discrimination legislation). We hope that by now it is clear that the steps which follow the second-order judgement are, in an important sense, inconsequential. In terms of the best use of Foucault's methods we are writing about here, it does not matter what content is put into the steps after the second-order judgement has done its work. What Inzammam makes of the 'hidden meaning' of *The Care of the Self* is, for us, of no great moment. Our concern is with the fact that he feels compelled to make anything of it at all, indeed that he feels compelled to track down such a beast as a 'hidden meaning'. Inzammam makes a second-order judgement the moment he moves away from accepting the appearance of Foucault's book as a compilation of details about Roman life, the moment his mind wants more, in his case a Marxian-influenced 'deep' meaning. At this point an aspect of the object being investigated – the supposed 'class' division between Roman techniques of the self – is granted a status – not necessarily 'cause' but certainly 'important feature' – which draws its authority from another investigation – any one or group of Marx's investigations. A judgement made previously – by Marx, but, as we've indicated, by many others before him as well – is exercised.

It's worth reminding you again that you should not expect your mind to ever stop wanting more. What we're urging here is that you make the effort, not that you succeed. It is through the attempt that you can at least succeed in the far less ambitious goal of being as sceptical as possible in regard to all political arguments. If you can check yourself to even a limited extent in the habit of making second-order judgements, you are well on the way to being properly sceptical in regard to political arguments in others' work and, more importantly, in your own. As such you are far less likely to fall into the trap of placing limits on the historicisation involved in Foucaultian scholarship, the trap at the heart of this chapter. Inzammam would not make the political claims he makes if he could curb his habit of second-order judgement; he would instantly be more sceptical and hence he would be in a much better position to dodge the trap of limiting historicisation.

Another example

Let's work quickly through one more example and then leave you with another exercise to complete the chapter. We'll deal with Jenny's reading of *The Care of the Self* as a reading group text and we'll hand on to you Zeeha's reading of it. Jenny's French theory reading group has arrived at *The Care of the Self* immediately after working through some texts in the tradition of Lacanian psychoanalysis. The group is bringing some interesting insights to Foucault's text in the light of this intellectual exercise.

At this point we must stress the care needed in dealing with the sorts of examples we (and you, if you are tackling the exercises diligently) are working through here. There is a real danger that you might take what we said about Inzammam and what we are about to say about Jenny and her reading group colleagues as licence for a sort of anti-intellectualism: if allowing pre-read authors like Marx to be the bearer of second-order judgements is a problem, perhaps it's best to avoid intellectual influences altogether and just go with our own reactions to the texts we read. While there are a couple of bizarre precedents in the history of theorising for such a move – Auguste Comte and Herbert Spencer (over a hundred years apart) practised a type of 'cerebral hygiene' (in Comte's compelling phrase) to try to free their minds from the 'pollution' of other writers' thoughts (Ritzer 1992: 16, 36) – this is not at all the direction we are promoting in this book. We strongly encourage Inzammam in reading the sociological classics and Jenny and her friends in reading widely in recent French theory. In targeting the problems created by second-order judgements we are not in any way seeking to limit the amount of reading good students do. Indeed, one of the by-products of the way we handle the Pyrrhonian heritage is an almost unfettered eclecticism. Treating seriously the proposition that we cannot know even that we cannot know means accepting all intellectual influences with the same sceptical acceptance of how things are. Taking exception to second-order judgements and their effects does not equate with taking exception to intellectual influences *per se*; it simply (or complexly) means treating them with sceptical respect.

Jenny, like Inzammam, accepts Foucault's history at face value on first reading but then she too habitually performs another reading. For Jenny this is necessary not because of a training in making overt political points – we will see shortly that the political arguments which follow Jenny's second-order judging are much more subtle than those which follow Inzammam's – but because she and her friends find French theory so foreign. Every text they have dealt with in the reading group has seemed impenetrable to them on first reading. They have had to work very hard on each occasion to 'make sense' of what they read. This has been especially true in the case of the psychoanalytic texts they have just put aside to deal with *The Care of the Self*. Where Inzammam and his class-mates have learned boldly to push ahead and impose political meanings on the texts they meet, Jenny's group has learned almost the exact opposite – to find meaning in the texts is a difficult and painstaking business, requiring an ethic of trying not to impose Anglophone values on a French text, an ethic only partially helped by familiarity with the French language (the group has become wary of any Francophone members who assume an attitude of superiority to those without such familiarity). Jenny habitually performs a subsequent reading of Foucault's text because she has an expectation that this text must be 'difficult' in the way all other 'French theory' texts are 'difficult'. It is in this way that Jenny allows second-order judgements to creep in and on the basis of them she and her friends make subtle ahistorical claims about theory and the way it should be handled. For example, they claim that Foucault can and should be read as part of a French intellectual movement – beginning with the Revolution and including nineteenth-century romanticism as well as twentieth-century traditions in feminism and psychoanalysis – concerned with the freedom of the individual.

In discussing this error we again stress that we are not disputing the truth of Jenny and her friends' ahistorical political claims: whether they are true or false is beside the point. Remember, such claims are not part of good Foucaultian scholarship and we try simply to show how this error can be avoided. And just as we acknowledged the inevitability of students making political points about the general exercise of power in society, so we must acknowledge the inevitability of at least some of them making political points about the much more particular use of power involved in techniques of reading and 'doing' theory. We here must repeat our exhortation that students learn to separate such claims from productive readings of Foucault's histories, to put them into a separate category of intellectual existence and try to use Foucault's methods without exercising this category (of course, it should hardly need repeating, they will never succeed in this completely; it's the attempt which is crucial). Let's again identify the moment when the second-order judgements raise their heads such that we can easily take the second step of isolating the ahistorical political claims.

In this case, the moment of the first appearance of second-order judgements is not the moment when the subtle political claims are made – not
when the group proposes *The Care of the Self* as the latest in a long line of
books about the freedom of the individual. Here again the second-order
judgements tend to sneak in, this time under the cloak not so much of a
mysterious figure as of a mysterious foreignness – the foreignness of the
French theoretical tradition. The result, however, is very similar – second-
order judging leads straight to the search for hidden meaning. Before we
elaborate this slightly, we need to defend 'the French theoretical tradition'
in the way we defended Marx.

While it is certainly the case that many individual French authors have
deliberately fostered the idea that there is an air of impenetrability about
their particular writings and the tradition from which they come (and
Foucault himself is occasionally guilty of this in remarks in his interviews),
these authors cannot be said to have invented this habit. Again we could
return to some ancient debates, this time about meaning, to find early
examples of this habit, though we would probably have more joy if we
looked at the Christian tradition of exegesis, the idea of working hard to
discover true meaning in a sacred text, but yet again we must remind you
that such an investigation is well beyond the scope of this book.

The technique of reading employed by Jenny and the other members of
her reading group relies for its force on this idea of the impenetrability of
certain texts. They have learned this habit as good scholarship. 'Always
look beneath the surface,' Jenny has taught herself, with plenty of prompting from her teachers and from the other group members. 'I can find deep
meanings if I look hard enough.' This is true, but it also a judgement Jenny
is importing into her reading.

The judgement, remember, is that there is something there, something
hidden, not so much that the something has any particular quality. We say
again, the steps that follow the second-order judgement are, in an important sense, inconsequential. In terms of the best use of Foucault's methods,
the content put into the steps after the second-order judgement has paid
its visit is of no interest to us. What Jenny makes of the 'hidden meaning'
of *The Care of the Self* is of no great moment. Our concern is with the fact
that she feels compelled to make anything of it, that she feels she must
look for 'hidden meaning'. Jenny makes a second-order judgement the
moment she moves away from accepting the appearance of Foucault's
book as a compilation of details about Roman life, the moment her mind
wants more, in her case a 'French' 'deep' meaning about the freedom of
individuals. At this point an aspect of the object being investigated – the
'quest for freedom' 'contained in' Roman techniques of the self – is granted
a status – not necessarily 'cause' but certainly 'important feature' – which
draws its authority from another investigation – any one or group of
French investigations conducted in the name of such a quest. A judgement
made previously – by many others – is exercised.

Why not exhort yourself one more time: check yourself to even a limited extent in the habit of making second-order judgements and you are well on the way to being properly sceptical, you are far less likely to fall into the trap of placing limits on the historicisation involved in Foucaultian scholarship. Jenny would not make the subtle political claims she makes if she could curb her habit of second-order judgement; she would instantly be more sceptical and hence she would be in a much better position to dodge the trap of limiting historicisation.

Let's consider this error in more detail.

EXERCISE 1.2

Consider the following description of Zeeha's reading of *The Care of the Self* and identify the point at which she first relies on a second-order judgement, describing this judgement in your own words.

Like Jenny and Inzammam, Zeeha accepts Foucault's history at face value on first reading but then also habitually performs another reading. Zeeha, like Jenny but unlike Inzammam, is not out to make overt political points. She seeks only to find some common link between the various techniques of the self Foucault describes as part of her quest to find a common logic behind Roman punishments. She has looked at many texts on Roman life with this in mind. On each occasion Zeeha has tried very hard to find hints about the 'real feelings' of Romans. Somewhat like Jenny, she has come to believe that textual analysis is a difficult and painstaking business. Zeeha habitually performs a subsequent reading of Foucault's text because she has an expectation that this text must be 'difficult' in the way all other texts about Roman life are 'difficult'. On the basis of this, Zeeha is quietly claiming that Foucault's book can and should be read as one of a group of texts about the 'real feelings' of Romans.

Now, bearing in mind that it is unnecessary to dispute the truth of Zeeha's quiet ahistorical political claim, and remembering that Zeeha has learned this habit as good scholarship (she too tells herself, 'Always look beneath the surface,' and, 'I can find deep meanings if I look hard enough') please outline, as simply as you can (in about 750 words), the method by which this error can be avoided.

2

'My head is spinning; doesn't history have to be more orderly than this?'

CONTENTS

'But the fact that the Greeks smiled on sex between men and boys two and a half thousand years ago says nothing about the thinking behind the new legislation.'

Curtly was starting to feel hemmed in. This classroom discussion had started well for him. He'd felt confident and knowledgeable, using what he'd learned from a recent encounter with Foucault in a manner that he thought was marking him out as intelligent. This line of objection from one of the other students was unexpected as well as unwelcome. He tried another tack.

'Well, let's leave the Greeks then and talk about the discourse of homosexuality in the nineteenth century.'

He didn't get far with this line of argument before he found himself confronted by not just the one but now two objectors; he had to fight off the fear of a conspiracy against him.

'Oh Curtly, that's no more relevant than your Greek example.'

'And not only that, but you're jumping around the centuries wildly . . . that's not going to convince anyone.'

Curtly held his breath hoping the teacher would step in on his behalf and put his detractors in their place. No such luck. She even joined in, apparently keen to become objector number three.

'Perhaps people are being too harsh on you,' she observed, her condescending tone shattering his vision of himself as the domineering but cool intellectual. 'I think your references to power might prove useful to our discussion, but it would help if you didn't bandy around terms like "archaeology" and "genealogy".'

Curtly had assumed that everyone knew what these terms meant and the thought that he might now be called on to define them filled him with dread. His brain kept asking him, 'How on earth do I get out of this swamp – "power, knowledge, discourse, archaeology and genealogy"; only this morning it looked like firm ground.'

Curtly needs our help.

Archaeology, genealogy and discourse are the tools Foucault uses to give some order to history at the same time as giving history the power–knowledge twist that makes the Foucaultian approach so distinctive. Learning to handle these tools with care is the key to avoiding the swamp into which Curtly is sinking. Before we deal in turn with each of these tools, we need briefly to develop a couple of the points from the previous chapter, by way of a reminder of both the importance of history for those seeking to use Foucault's methods and, at the same time, the unusual character of Foucaultian histories.

The first point for brief development is that while Foucault's historical methods are crucially about problematisation, this should not make you anxious. It is important that you learn how to turn your position of uncertainty into a virtue. A compatriot of Foucault's, Jean-François Lyotard, gives you the strongest of hints:

> One writes before knowing what there is to say and how to say it, to find out if possible. . . . Obviously the only interesting thing for the philosopher is to think what he can't manage to think: without that. . . . I wonder what the hell he'd be doing. (Lyotard as quoted in Bennington 1988: 103–4)

Let's take this a little more slowly. We can unpack the statement about problematisation. Foucault's approach to history is to select a *problem* rather than an historical period for investigation. The problem might be 'How did the prison emerge as the major form of punishment?', or 'How did sex come to be seen as so important in terms of who we are?' But, whatever, it is crucial that we allow our investigations of a problem to surprise us. Foucault's methods involve the generation of surprising stories (we elaborate on this below).

Let's make sure this point is clear. The following exercise is designed to make sure you appreciate the difference between a problem-based and a period-based approach to history.

EXERCISE 2.1

Write a list of three historical periods that might make sensible topics for investigation (for example, 1939–45 as the period of the Second World War). Now try to think how you could start work in these three areas using a problem-based approach (for example, how did National Socialism in Germany become linked with world domination?). What happens to the historical time period of your investigation?

The second point for brief development concerns the perpetual nature of Foucault's histories. You'll remember that we urged you not to let history stop, not to let history settle on a patch of sensibleness in a field of strangeness. Our development of this point involves something of a qualification. While we must not let history stop we should always bear in mind that in checking ourselves in this manner we are thereby making use of an analytical tool. In other words 'not letting history stop' is not an end in itself. Unfortunately some scholars who have taken up a version of this method, under the label 'deconstruction', treat the actual 'deconstruction' as the only goal, so in their case 'not letting history stop' has definitely become an end in itself. We should be wary of the oblivion of such academicism, by which we mean that if we focus only upon 'not letting history stop', as an end in itself, our projects will be relevant only to those few other souls trapped in this academic wonderland (a fate which sometimes befalls this type of 'deconstructionist'). (The term 'deconstruction', most closely associated with the name of Jacques Derrida, is difficult to define. It refers to a close and critical analysis of texts in an attempt to lay bare their hidden allegiances and affiliations, traditionally concentrating on the binary structures of meaning of western metaphysics. It should be noted that we are not dealing here with the full picture of Derridean deconstructionism, which has a very sound intellectual pedigree, only with a crude, limited but popular, gloss of it.)

Our answer to the crucial question, 'When, then, is the right moment to unleash our awareness that "not letting history stop" is an analytical device?' is 'All the time.' The Pyrrhonian scepticism at the heart of our Foucaultian method gives us the all-important sceptical distance from our investigations such that, if we are using it properly, we can be confident that while we are not letting history stop, we are aware of not doing so as an intellectual move related to our investigation. The object of our investigation – be it sexuality, crime, punishment, madness, or any other – is not allowed to quietly rot while we engage in an orgy of self-congratulation about not letting history stop. We can be confident that we are not letting it stop in order to produce a better investigation of our object rather than because it is a worthwhile intellectual achievement in itself.

Archaeology

Some basics

Archaeology is our first Foucaultian 'ordering tool' for discussion. In *The Archaeology of Knowledge* Foucault engages in a minute dissection of his own vocabulary. In discussing archaeology as a tool, he says that the analysis of the statement as it occurs in the archive is his main concern (1972: 79ff). In addition, Foucault points out that archaeology 'describes discourses as practices specified in the element of the archive' (1972: 131), the archive being 'the general system of the formation and transformation of statements' (1972: 130). Foucault's terminology here reminds us that his approach is *historical*, although it must be said he is sometimes too keen to distinguish between 'archaeology' and 'history'. This emphasis is confirmed when he suggests that to follow his method one is necessarily engaging in historical work, conceived of in his own idiosyncratic way: 'the archaeological description of discourses is deployed in the dimension of a general history' (1972: 164). Reading between the lines here, Foucault is linking his work to an existing tradition of French historiography (the Annales School as well as the historical analyses of the sciences put together by Bachelard and Canguilhem). Foucault emphasises the general history; the approach to which this is opposed is the total history. The total history looks for overarching principles which govern the development of an epoch; by contrast, the general history eschews the 'totalising' theme, concentrating instead on describing differences, transformations, continuities, mutations, and so forth (Foucault 1972: 9–10). It is worth citing Mitchell Dean at some length here to make this distinction clear:

> A total history seeks a governing principle of a civilisation, epoch or society, which accounts for its coherence; it seeks to establish an homogeneous network of relations and causality across a clearly defined set of spatial and temporal co-ordinates; it imposes a totalistic form of transformation, and it is able to divide history into definite, cohesive, periods and stages. . . . A general history, on the other hand . . . seeks series, divisions, differences of temporality and level, forms of continuity and mutation, particular types of transitions and events, possible relations and so on. A general history would be non-reductive, non-totalising, one which specifies its own terrain, the series it constitutes, and the relations between them: . . . [It] opens up an attention to detail, grain, and complexity, and the specification of form of relation which is indispensable if [we are] to move beyond caricatures of historical periodisation passing for a science of social development. (1994: 93–4)

Archaeology helps us to explore the networks of what is said, and what can be seen in a set of social arrangements: in the conduct of an archaeology, one finds out something about the visible in 'opening up' statements and something about the statement in 'opening up visibilities'. This all sounds fairly obscure, but an example might make this clearer. In his discussion of the birth of the prison, *Discipline and Punish* (1977), Foucault's central task is to show how the prison as a form of visibility (a visible thing) produces statements about criminality, while statements about criminality produce forms of visibility which reinforce prison. You can take from this example the idea in Foucault that statements and visibilities *mutually condition* each other.

Later in this chapter we discuss the notion of discourse in considerable detail. We must now jump ahead of ourselves for a moment as our next point about archaeology concerns its relation to discourse. One of Foucault's primary concerns is to investigate what he calls the discourse of the emergence of 'Man', not in terms of 'truth', but in terms of history. For him this necessitates investigation of the history of the statement and, as such, he makes continual recourse to the *archive*. We can say, in the light of this, that archaeology is the process of investigating the archives of discourse.

The waters are starting to run deep. Curtly may not be the only one thinking this is heavy. Let's look in on Steffi. A far more cautious type than Curtly, she has kept quiet in her Sociology class despite her intense interest in the discussions on Foucault currently dominating this class. One of her former boyfriends is a postgraduate scholar at another university. Steffi bumped into him about a year ago and was relieved that he seemed genuinely interested in what she was reading (she'd found him condescending towards her intellectual pursuits when they were together). It was in this context that she really valued the advice he'd offered about taking up Foucault: 'If you want to understand Foucault, it's best to leave the trendy studies of sex and prisons until after you've worked your way through *The Order of Things* and *The Archaeology of Knowledge*.' In the intervening year she had indeed worked her way carefully through these two tomes. Nonetheless, she still felt ill at ease around discussions of Foucault. She thought of giving this former boyfriend a call, but she didn't want him to think she was 'interested' again, so she battled on alone. Steffi wasn't so much worried about not understanding what she'd read – she felt she had a reasonable grasp of most of the concepts discussed even though at times she had felt her head swimming – as worried that she didn't know what to do with her understanding. Every class discussion about Foucault left her with the same problem – how to make Foucault useful.

This is where we come back into the picture. In addressing Steffi's immediate problem we can also help Curtly; he is being too bold whereas Steffi is being too timid. We propose two principles of archaeological research which are derived from the insistence on conducting a general rather than a total history:

1 In seeking to provide no more than a description of regularities, differences, transformations, and so on, archaeological research is non-interpretive.
2 In eschewing the search for authors and concentrating instead on statements (and visibilities), archaeological research is non-anthropological.

We also shortly offer some points about archaeological research in action, but first we must make sure these principles are clear.

The first principle is pointedly Pyrrhonian. To say that archaeological research is non-interpretive is to say that it avoids judgements. We covered this ground in the previous chapter and warned that avoiding judgement is not as easy as it might seem. We stress again, in this context, that it is the *attempt* to be non-interpretive that is important. The other aspect of this principle is equally Pyrrhonian. To say that archaeological research seeks to provide a description of regularities and so forth is to say that archaeological research is not only content to remain at the level of appearances, but that it has no time for any quest to go 'beyond' this level to find 'deeper meanings'.

The second principle is also Pyrrhonian but covers ground we did not cover in the previous chapter. In saying that archaeological research is non-anthropological, we are adding another dimension to the exhortation to concentrate on appearances. The principle exhorts us to concentrate on the appearances of statements and by implication to avoid the habit of seeking to source meaning in human beings. Foucault's archaeological method is, at least in part, a means to break this habit. This point will be echoed later when we discuss power.

Archaeology in action

In action archaeological research attempts at least seven things:

1 to chart the relation between the sayable and the visible;
2 to analyse the relation between one statement and other statements;
3 to formulate rules for the repeatability of statements (or, if you like, the use of statements);
4 to analyse the positions which are established between subjects – for the time being we can think of subjects as human beings – in regard to statements;
5 to describe 'surfaces of emergence' – places within which objects are designated and acted upon;
6 to describe 'institutions', which acquire authority and provide limits within which discursive objects may act or exist;
7 to describe 'forms of specification', which refer to the ways in which discursive objects are targeted. A 'form of specification' is a system for understanding a particular phenomenon with the aim of relating it to other phenomena.

Each of these seven 'tasks' of archaeological research needs slightly more discussion to render them clear points of instruction for you (and for Curtly and Steffi). A single example is the best way to tackle this. An archaeological analysis of schooling attempts at least seven things:

1   The attempt to understand the relation between the sayable and the visible focuses on those sets of statements and arrangements that make up the school – instructions to principals and teachers, instructions from them to pupils, statements about the curriculum, the school buildings involved, the timetabling arrangements, and so on. Knowledge is composed of the sayable and the visible, or words and things. In our example of schooling, we need to attend to both what is said (theories of learning, theories of discipline, etc.) and what is visible (buildings, blackboards, instruments of punishment, etc.). The crucial point here is that Foucault draws our attention to the dynamic, mutually conditioning relationship between words and things.

2   The attempt to analyse the relation between one statement and other statements focuses on the *ordering* of statements such that those to principals and teachers from government authorities provide the framework for those from principals and teachers to pupils, and so on. Investigation should focus on how a system of statements works.

3   The attempt to formulate rules for the repeatability of statements focuses on the procedures used by government authorities, principals, teachers, parents, and so forth, to deploy some statements – say, statements concerned to increase discipline – rather than others that may be equally feasible, such as statements about the freedom of individual children to choose. In particular, what is of concern here are the ways in which certain statements (for example, concerning discipline) can come to be repeated. This reflects a point we made earlier that it isn't the case in the Foucaultian approach that 'anything goes'. We need to examine what precisely it is that makes certain statements repeatable, to be part of the true, if you will permit such flowery language for a moment.

4   The attempt to analyse the positions which are established between subjects in regard to statements focuses on the way statements produce subject positions – ways of being and acting that human beings can take up – such as 'principal', 'teacher', 'inspector', 'parent', 'pupil' and, more intricately, 'slow learner', 'genius', 'good teacher', 'encouraging parent', and so on.

5   The attempt to describe 'surfaces of emergence' focuses on 'the school' or 'the family' as a domain. Within this domain, educational psychology, for example, can determine the 'proper' development of children as special types of educational subject (pupils, slow learners, geniuses, etc.), and can act on children as raw materials (children as family members, playful individuals, etc.).

6   The attempt to describe 'institutions', which acquire authority and provide limits within which discursive objects may act, focuses again

on the school, which delimits the range of activities of discursive objects (remembering that institutions are usually 'places of visibility' it is at this point that our analysis would explore the architectural features of school in a bid to understand the contribution some spatial arrangements – special seating, special rooms, special desks, observation spaces, etc. – make to the operation of these institutions).

7   The attempt to describe 'forms of specification', which refer to the ways in which discursive objects are targeted, focuses on the systematic ways that phenomena are rendered accessible to us. So, for example, educational psychology gives us a vocabulary and a series of concepts that enable us to get the measure of the schoolchild.

You may have noticed that we cheated a little here. We drew up a possible archaeology for education, but, of course, what was missing was our problem. But we think we can leave that to you.

EXERCISE 2.2

First of all, please think of some problems like those you generated for the last exercise in using the problem-based approach. Now use the list above to write down what an archaeology of one of your problems would need to discover. Don't worry if you cannot cover all seven steps (if you can, then the problem probably doesn't need researching!). Finally, use this framework to think about how an archaeology would be constructed. Please write no more than 1,000 words.

In more general terms we can characterise archaeology as a response by Foucault to a series of theoretical problems that were very much of the 1950s and 1960s. Foucault's archaeological work is sometimes considered to be part of the wider structuralist tradition which emerged from this period. Leaving aside the question of whether this is an accurate description, it is fair to say that, like the structuralists, Foucault was seeking at the time to respond to, and to break free from, the traditions of phenomenology and existentialism. Archaeology is a methodological device that owes much to Heidegger, Bachelard and Canguilhem, in that it is anti-humanist and non-Marxist (it is similar to Althusser's work in being anti-humanist, but very different in being non-Marxist).

We include this characterisation of archaeology in terms of its intellectual heritage not only to help you situate it in terms of the work of figures and traditions you may have dealt with (or at least heard of) but also because it is important to our story. It helps mark some distinctions between archaeology and genealogy.

Genealogy

As Foucault often discusses in some of his later interviews and lectures (the piece translated as 'Two Lectures' [1980b] is an especially good source), in the 1970s he became very keen to develop methodological weapons to help him with his account of power (to which we return later). Genealogy was his main achievement in this quest. Genealogy (the term itself is borrowed from Nietzsche, though Foucault's methodological development is different from Nietzsche's) was often promoted by Foucault as a kind of successor to archaeology. Despite this, genealogy maintains many of the essential ingredients of archaeology, including, paradoxically, the examination of bodies of statements in the archive. However, Foucault added to it a new concern with the analysis of power, a concern which manifests itself in the 'history of the present'.

As we saw in the previous chapter, Foucault's genealogy as 'history of the present' is not an attempt to impose second-order political judgements. No, it is of a different character, niggardly rather than judgemental. Genealogy concerns itself with 'disreputable origins and unpalatable functions', as Nikolas Rose puts it (1984: Introduction). It is, in other words, a methodological device with the same effect as a precocious child at a dinner party: genealogy makes the older guests at the table of intellectual analysis feel decidedly uncomfortable by pointing out things about their origins and functions that they would rather remain hidden. For example, Foucault's genealogy of psychiatry makes psychiatrists feel uncomfortable by pointing out that the origins and functions of this science are far from the noble enterprise dedicated to the service of humanity that the official histories would have us believe – 'Couldn't the interweaving of effects of power and knowledge be grasped with greater certainty in the case of a science as 'dubious' as psychiatry?' (Foucault 1980b: 109). Foucault famously annoyed psychiatrists by his claim, half-serious, that psychiatry was born out of a desire to fill the empty leper houses with a new sort of outcast – the mad person. His genealogies of other formal knowledge areas – penology, medicine, psychology, sexology, etc. – have the same effect.

It's worth spending a little time at this juncture, with considerable help from James Butterfield (1996), clarifying the connections, only hinted at so far, between Pyrrhonian scepticism and Foucault's genealogical method. Foucault sees modern philosophy (since Kant) in two distinct camps. On the one hand are those philosophers dedicated to an 'analytics of truth' (Foucault 1988a: 95), those who seek to find the essential rationality of the Enlightenment and preserve it (Foucault 1984: 43). Probably the most famous modern exponent of this position is Jürgen Habermas. On the other hand is the camp – and Foucault sees himself in this group – concerned rather with an 'ontology of ourselves' (Foucault 1988a: 95), with explorations of the 'contemporary limits of the necessary' (Foucault 1984: 43).

Foucault is clear that this second tradition involves no judging:

> [I]t's amazing how people like judging. Judgement is being passed everywhere, all the time. Perhaps it is one of the simplest things mankind has been given to do. And you know very well that the last man, when radiation has finally reduced his last enemy to ashes, will sit down behind some rickety table and begin the trial of the individual responsible. . . . I can't help but dream about a kind of criticism that would not try to judge. (1988b: 326)

Genealogy is, perhaps, one product of this dreaming. It does not judge as it rudely flushes out assumptions; claims about what is right and what is wrong have no place here; Foucault wants to make 'facile gestures difficult' (1988c: 155).

As with Pyrrhonism, this branch of philosophy is ultimately inward-looking. Foucault tells us that we must work on our 'selves', 'one must take responsibility for inventing or producing one's own self' (1984: 39–42). Unlike the passivity of the Pyrrhonian goal of imperturbability, however, Foucault seeks maximum individual freedom by a more active route. Taken to its extreme, genealogy targets us, our 'selves': it seems we are meant to see beyond the contingencies that have made each of us what we are in order that we might think in ways that we have not thought and be in ways that we have not been; it is a tool we might use in a quest for freedom. Foucault wants us constantly to extend the limits of the necessary, to use this 'critical ontology of ourselves' by way of 'testing' the 'limits that we may go beyond, and thus as work carried out by ourselves upon ourselves as free beings' (1984: 47). This aspect of genealogy is thus not so much about knowledge as about 'an agitation within' towards the capacity for self-reinvention.

You may be disappointed (or you may be thrilled) to learn that we cannot take you any further on this journey of self-exploration. As with our handling of Pyrrhonism, we must recognise the limits of our venture; we are only prepared to go as far as our methodological inquiry takes us. As we acknowledged in the case of Pyrrhonism, this is, relatively speaking, not very far. But as we also pointed out when setting the limits to our inquiry into scepticism, the possibility of an exploration of a 'way of life' lies at the end of most philosophical roads. We are not being shockingly conservative (at least we don't believe we are) in stopping a long way short of this 'end of the road', and nor is Foucault being wildly radical in wanting to go further. As he himself concedes, to pursue a critical philosophical ethos has been something of a tradition of philosophers since Kant, a tradition that includes 'Hegel, through Nietzsche and Max Weber, to the Frankfurt School' (Foucault 1988a: 95). It is in line with the recognition of the limits of our endeavour that we return to the more mundane methodological issue of the distinctions between genealogy and archaeology.

Genealogy also establishes its difference from archaeology in its approach to discourse. Where archaeology provides us with a snapshot, a slice through the discursive nexus, genealogy pays attention to the processual aspects of the web of discourse – its ongoing character (Foucault 1981b: 70–1).

Perhaps it occurs to you at this point, as it occurs to us and has occurred to other scholars as well, that a lot can be gained by keeping archaeology and genealogy together. There has been much dispute over the relation between archaeology and genealogy in Foucault's work (some scholars claim to be archaeologists, some genealogists), but we maintain that, despite his occasional efforts to distance himself from the terminology of *The Archaeology of Knowledge*, Foucault himself regarded the two methods as complementary, distinguished only by their differing emphases on 'historical slice' (however extended that slice might be) or 'historical process' (Foucault 1978a, 1981b: 70–1; Kremer-Marietti 1985), that is, the way they approach discourse.

Perhaps Foucault offers his clearest distinction between the two when he says:

> If we were to characterise it in two terms, then 'archaeology' would be the appropriate methodology of this analysis of local discursivities, and 'genealogy' would be the tactics whereby, on the basis of the descriptions of these local discursivities, the subjected knowledges which were thus released would be brought into play. (1980b: 85)

What we take from this quote is that archaeology can be understood as Foucault's method; genealogy is not so much a method as a way of putting archaeology to work, a way of linking it to our present concerns. We might think of genealogy as the *strategic* development of archaeological research (see also Foucault 1981a; Bevis et al. 1993; Dean 1994: 32–4).

There we go again, talking about discourse before we have properly introduced you to it. Before demystifying discourse, however, you have an exercise to do to help Curtly and Steffi test their knowledge of archaeology and genealogy.

EXERCISE 2.3

Given that Curtly is a 'rush-ahead, get to the latest soonest' sort of person and Steffi is a cautious 'build your knowledge from the ground up' character, it won't surprise you to learn that Curtly wants to quickly pack his knowledge of archaeology into the cupboard and put his faith in the little he's learned about genealogy, whereas Steffi feels archaeology needs to be maintained and genealogy taken with a pinch of salt.

By coincidence they have each been asked to write an essay on governmental responses to the Paris cholera outbreak of 1832 and its aftermath. They have been given the following details about this event (taken from Kendall and Wickham 1996: 209–12):

[T]he disease [marched] from India in 1826, through Russia in 1830, through Poland, Hungary, Prussia, Germany, Austria and England in 1831, and arriv[ed] in Paris in the spring of 1832 – despite many popular theories suggesting that the superiority of French civilisation would somehow provide immunity against the scourge. By the time the disease had run its course in the city, some eighteen thousand Parisians were dead. The 1832 epidemic led the authorities to add two governmental health tactics to the Classical health measures of quarantine at the ports and local health committees. Rabinow summarises these two new tactics by the terms 'sanitary measures' and 'health measures'. The former aimed to prevent the contact of bodies and substances; the latter, in line with the theory that disease was transmitted through the air, aimed to target and to break up unhealthy locales. . . .

More and more rational targetings of the population were set in play . . . . Such attempts to build a causal story of cholera . . . proved inconclusive, however, and 'social conditions', theorised per inhabitant and per building, proved a more fruitful source of ideas. . . .

Parisian officials, inspired by their faith in the sorts of scientific knowledges that study of the epidemic was producing, were not slow to impose their governmental authority on urban cultural life – many dwellings and popular public areas were condemned, many buildings were forcibly whitewashed, the character of streets was fundamentally altered by the provision of fountains and paving, public facilities like hospitals, prisons and barracks were subject to a reorganisation of their various regimens of diet and clothing. However . . . government . . . involves a complex mix of success and failure which often involves the ingredient known widely, but fairly loosely, by the name 'resistance'.

Cholera was not, of course, the only problem Paris had to face.

> By the 1850s, the conditions of housing, health, circulation, and infrastructure (water and sewage [sic]) in Paris were appalling. Paris had very few large streets . . . and they were poorly linked, uneven, and crammed with traffic. . . . Paris's population had increased from 580,000 in 1805 to 1,274,000 in 1851 and would rise to over 2,000,000 by the end of the Second Empire. . . . Cholera reappeared in 1847, 1848, and 1849. The Saint-Simonian Victor Considérant commented darkly in 1848 that Paris was 'a great manufactory of putrefaction in which poverty, plague, and disease labour in concert, and air and sunlight barely enter. Paris is a foul hole where plants wilt and perish and four out of seven die within a year'. (Rabinow 1989: 73–4)

In 1853, in a bid to rectify the situation, Louis Napoleon turned to Baron Georges Haussmann:

> Haussmann approached the city as a technical object to be worked on, improved, and regulated. To this end, one of his first efforts was to establish a detailed and comprehensive plan of Paris. The fact that it took a year to complete indicates the degree of specialization, administrative hierarchy, and technical proficiency demanded for such a task. . . . The top priorities were

> hygiene and circulation. . . . Circulation meant opening wide
> avenues, connecting them to squares or places, and establishing
> further connections with smaller arteries. (Rabinow 1989: 77)

The extent of Haussmann's rebuilding is remarkable. Fifty-seven miles of new straight wide streets were built. The number of gas-lamps was dramatically increased, and they were kept burning all night. The provision of municipal parks was a top priority; while Paris had just 47 acres of parkland in 1850, by 1870 it was able to boast 4,500. Haussmann also addressed the dire water and sewerage problems. While he did not quite achieve his ambition to supply running water to every Parisian household, by convincing Napoleon of the worth of the Roman aqueduct model, he came very close.

We can safely assume that Curtly and Steffi are now well enough versed in the ways of Foucaultian scholarship that neither needs reminding that history is at the heart of the use of both archaeology and genealogy.

Please consider the following lists of techniques discussed so far as aspects of the tools of archaeology and genealogy, then write a brief plan each for Curtly and Steffi to help with their essays (you need write no more than about 1,000 words in total). In your plan for Curtly's essay, concentrate on genealogy; in your plan for Steffi's essay, use only archaeology.

Archaeology

- describes statements in the archive, statements covering the sayable and the visible;
- describes regularities of statements in a non-interpretive manner (content to remain at the level of appearances, eschewing any quest to go 'beyond' this level to find 'deeper meanings');
- describes statements in a non-anthropological manner, as a means of avoiding the search for authors (again remaining at the level of appearances – the appearances of statements – to avoid the habit of seeking to source meaning in human beings);
- analyses the relation between one statement and other statements;
- formulates rules for the repeatability of statements – what allows certain statements to recur;
- analyses the positions which are established between subjects in regard to statements;
- describes 'surfaces of emergence' – or places within which objects are made objects in discourse;
- describes the institutions which acquire authority and provide limits within which discursive objects may act;
- describes the 'forms of specification' in which discursive objects are targeted.

Genealogy

- describes statements but with an emphasis on power;
- introduces power through a 'history of the present', concerned with 'disreputable origins and unpalatable functions', making the older guests at the table of intellectual analysis feel decidedly uncomfortable by pointing out things about their origins and functions that they would rather remain hidden;
- describes statements as an ongoing process, rather than as a snapshot of the web of discourse;
- concentrates on the strategic use of archaeology to answer problems about the present.

We can put it off no longer; it is now time to try to unravel some of the mystery of the seemingly most Foucaultian of notions – discourse. You'll see that it is quite manageable and far from mysterious if chewed in digestible pieces.

Discourse

Some basics

The best place to start our account of discourse is to reassure you that one of the main features of Foucault's handling of this notion is fairly straightforward, something you have almost certainly met and understood already – that discourses are productive: medical discourses about 'folly' and 'unreason' produce the mentally ill person, penological discourses produce the criminal, discourses on sex produce sexuality, and so on. However, we shouldn't rush in too quickly. We need to be a little careful as this Foucaultian approach to discourse is sometimes taken to mean that before the existence of these discourses, there was no mental illness, criminality, sexuality, and so on. This line of thinking should be resisted.

To take just one of these examples, we can say sexuality only emerged from the eighteenth century when a variety of strategies of power and knowledge applied themselves to the field of sex, but before sexuality, there was not a void. A series of deployments of alliance based on kinship ties, deployments of the flesh based on Christianity, deployments of the uses of pleasure based on self-mastery, all may be taken as precursors of 'sexuality'. Sex may be subject to certain physiological limitations in the modern era of discourses of sexuality, but before this era sex obviously existed: it was the raw material for the sexuality with which we are now familiar. But don't jump too far the other way either – this is not to say that sex exists in a purely non-discursive realm and was simply waiting for discourse to come along to fashion it. We return to the question of what

Foucault sees outside discourse later. For now it is enough to tell you that while he does not propose discourse as all-encompassing, his account of the non-discursive is certainly not as crude as to suggest that things like sex exist in a purely non-discursive realm.

This may seem an odd time to introduce you to doubts about the use of the term 'discourse' itself, but introduce you to them we must, for it would be almost impossible for you not to entertain such doubts yourselves sooner or later given what has happened to the term in the last decade or so. The term 'discourse' has gained a wide contemporary currency and is perhaps in danger of becoming all things to all people. The crucial thing here is to avoid the idea that it is a purely linguistic term (as in most incarnations of 'discourse analysis'). Discourse is not only about language.

In working through this point we are given a great deal of help by a Griffith University discussion document circulated by Ian Hunter in the early 1980s, appropriately titled 'Michel Foucault: Discourse versus Language' (this paper has never been published, though some points in it were later aired in Hunter 1989). Hunter makes the introductory point that

> Foucault's reformulation of the concept of discourse derives from his attempts to provide histories of knowledge which are not histories of what men and women have thought. Foucault's histories are not histories of ideas, opinions or influences nor are they histories of the way in which economic, political and social contexts have shaped ideas or opinions. Rather they are reconstructions of the *material conditions* of thought or 'knowledges'. They represent an attempt to produce what Foucault calls an *archaeology* of the material conditions of thought/knowledges, conditions which are not reducible to the idea of 'consciousness' or the idea of 'mind'. (Hunter n.d., emphasis in original)

Hunter develops this point by exploring Foucault's metaphor that discourse has no inside (in thought) and no outside (in things). Foucault is seeking to fragment what we usually understand as 'thinking', not to universalise it as 'thought'.

Discourse – no 'inside'

The insistence that there is no 'inside' is Foucault's way of telling us to forget the idea of a thinking process operating prior to the use of words and symbols in order to make their use possible. Hunter offers an example, combining Foucault's insights with those of the philosopher Ludwig Wittgenstein:

> [P]rior to our use of words we do *not* have mental acts/processes which are then 'expressed' in words. . . . [For example, consider] a simple mathematical discourse, a simple algebraic formula for expanding a series: $y = 2x + 5$; if $x = 2$, then the series runs 9, 23, 51, etc. [We urge you at this point to make sure you can follow this simple formula – $2 \times 2 + 5 = 9$; $2 \times 9 + 5 = 23$, etc. – before pushing on with Hunter's explanation.]

Now at any point in the expansion of this series, what does it mean to 'think' of the next number? Surely it means to perform the calculation (the discursive operation) which results in that number. There is no question of this discursive operation expressing my thought of the next number, a thought which exists independently of the operation of the mathematical discourse. For this to be the case it would have to be possible to think of the next number without performing the calculation. And this is not possible. . . . It is unintelligible because performing the calculation materially produces the criteria for what we will call 'the next number'. One doesn't think of the next number by some general faculty of recognition prior to being equipped – in a very straightforward sense in schools – with the techniques of algebra. (Hunter n.d., emphasis in original)

This example is ideal because it alerts us (and by 'us' we mean Curtly, Steffi, you and us) to the simple truth that knowledge goes on without us, a simple truth that is axiomatic with Foucault's methods. It is a simple truth that you will grasp quite easily if you carefully worked your way through what we had to say about Pyrrhonian scepticism in Chapter 1, but it is also a simple truth that needs a further example, one dealing with a narrative discourse rather that a mathematical one. Hunter does not let us down, turning to Foucault's (1978b) account of the discourse of confession contained in the first volume of *The History of Sexuality*:

Here, Foucault is making the same general point, namely, that consciousness of 'sins of the flesh' is not something that exists in the mind. Rather it is something that appears, historically, on the surface of an organization of techniques and statements. . . . Foucault demonstrates that confession, at the time of the church fathers, wasn't a particularly important church ritual. Indeed, up until the Renaissance, confession was more or less an annual event for Catholics. Foucault records that during the Renaissance a pressure emerges for confession to become much more frequent, to become (eventually) a weekly phenomenon, and he also records that what counts as a confession changes. The rules for making a confession, the structure of the confessional, the text put about for both penitent and confessors to learn, alter. And they alter in a way that privileges what we would now call 'sins of sexuality'. During the Renaissance sins of sexuality become the cardinal sins, the 'league ladder' of sins alters. Once gluttony and sloth were up there with sex but during the Renaissance sex becomes the big one and the important thing is that not only does sex as a sin, an act (as in adultery and fornication) become extremely important but also and for the first time, the possibility that one might sin in thought becomes important. (Hunter n.d.)

Hunter captures superbly the scope of Foucault's notion of discourse. Here we see discourse at work producing aspects of life to which a purely linguistic version of the notion would not have given us access.

Curtly is puzzled. He can take in these points from Hunter but wonders how they can be applied to anything. For him they are still simply points about Foucault, not points of method which he can use. He is being impatient. Steffi, as we've come to expect, puts more time into thinking through the implications of the points. She is able to apply them to a contemporary issue in which she has recently become involved, as something of a student activist: fees for tertiary education. Steffi is involved in an anti-fees group. Through her thinking she sees that the position she and her group have taken up is not a spontaneous opposition deriving from some notion of rights, as some of the group members argue. She realises that their position cannot be reached independently of mechanisms of political calculation, as if a political position could somehow magically form itself in their minds. As such she realises that it is futile to hope that others will take up or support their position spontaneously. It is the operation of the mechanisms – political parties, organised student groups, some university courses, some books, some newspapers, etc. – that allows her and her friends to point to the issue and to make arguments about it. The discourse of their opposition is more complex and more *material* than she previously understood and she now feels confident in urging that the group pay more attention to the mechanisms of calculation and less to the language of rights. Steffi starts to realise that if she wanted to do a Foucaultian analysis of this issue, she would need to understand (historically) how the mechanisms of calculation came to be formed. Sometimes Foucault refers to this type of work as uncovering the *conditions of possibility* for a knowledge or an historical event. You need not be too worried by this rather daunting phrase: all it suggests is that we need to describe the various bits and pieces that had to be in place to allow something else to be possible (and note here how this rather careful formulation allows you to avoid even the remotest sugges-tion that the emergent event or knowledge or whatever was *necessary*).

Returning to Hunter's characterisation of Foucault's notion, he argues that for Foucault, 'thought' is nothing special, not the product of some higher order called 'thinking'. Rather, 'thought' is the name given to 'the material surfaces of appearances' which result from the operation of 'a dis-persed collection of public historical apparatuses'. In line with this, an algebraic expansion of numbers, like other 'thoughts', is not the product of a private mental procedure carried out by more or less intelligent thinkers; it is the result of the operation of public apparatuses (in this case mainly maths teaching in schools). We cannot go beyond this discursive 'surface' to a 'deeper inside' of 'thought': the surface is all there is. We could say the same about 'thoughts' of sin and the operation of mechan-isms of confession.

> What Foucault is suggesting is that thinking doesn't reduce to anything; it has no essence, no simple character and there is nothing about it that distinguishes . . . [human beings] from beasts. Thinking is whatever we call thinking . . . all the things that have historically emerged from these public apparatuses. (Hunter n.d.)

Before we turn to the other half of Foucault's metaphor – that discourse has no 'outside' in things – we should set your mind at rest if you've been clever enough to yet again see the connections between this account of dis-course and the account of Pyrrhonian scepticism offered in the previous chapter. You're right of course: Foucault's notion of discourse is best handled as an extension of his Pyrrhonian approach to history.

Discourse – no 'outside'

Hunter ties Foucaultian discourse's lack of an 'outside' very closely to its lack of an 'inside':

> [O]ur use of words is not governed by the familiar notion of 'reference' . . . [I]t is the use of words (that is, the operation of definite forms of calculation . . .) that determines what will count as the properties of objects. For example, it would be fruitless to try to ground the meaning of $y = 2x + 4$ by pointing to the numbers that are its object. The reason being that operating the formula is *how* one points to the numbers. (Hunter n.d., emphasis in original)

Hunter reminds us again that Foucault is not universalising discourse here; he is, rather, fragmenting reference. 'He is attempting to break up *reference* into *domains of reference*, domains established by the operation of particular forms of calculation and types of statement that organise the diverse spaces in which particular types of object can appear' (Hunter n.d., emphasis in original).

This time Curtly is starting to catch on. Taking more time than he did previously, he formulates a useful example of his own. Thinking through the coming into being of a particular Act of government, one to do with the regulation of trade unions, a topic dear to Curtly's heart, he thinks through the operation of the discursive mechanisms involved – books, journal articles, newspaper reports, formal and informal discussions, court judgments, formal government proceedings, and so on. Curtly is aware that we cannot say that these mechanisms are governed by the procedures of trade unions, governments and employers which the Act oversees. He knows that we cannot ground the meaning of these procedures simply by pointing to the procedures because we can only point to them by operating the mechanisms. We can only recognise the domain of industrial law, Curtly continues, by the operation of the particular forms of calculation and recognition that organise the spaces in which the objects of industrial law appear and operate.

Here again we see the influence of Pyrrhonistic scepticism. Curtly is expounding the point well: we cannot go beyond the discursive surface of industrial law to a 'deeper outside' of industrial 'things'. Like other 'things', these industrial 'things' have no independent existence in a different realm to which industrial law must defer; they are the result of the operation of a public apparatus of law, the discourse of law. This is not to say that other discourses do not contest law's operation. The 'things' involved in the operation of this discourse of industrial law almost certainly resemble the 'things' involved in competing discourses – trade union activities that take place in non-legal settings, for example – and the subjects of these competing discourses – say, the trade union activists urging strikes rather than court actions – will almost certainly claim that the 'things' in their discursive field are more real than those in the industrial law field, but don't be fooled. If you've taken on enough of the sceptical distance we've been urging you to adopt, you'll see that whatever the claims made by the subjects of one discourse or another, none of them have access to a realm of non-discursive 'deeper' reality.

There is still room for the idea of the non-discursive – a very important idea for Foucault, as we indicated earlier – but not for the idea of the 'deeper' realm. We leave Ian Hunter's contribution at precisely the point at which we joined it, for he concludes with a reiteration of the theme that the term 'discourse' is a problem. He says it is the source of 'a major ambiguity and is a major weakness in *The Archaeology of Knowledge*'. Because of the use of the term 'discourse', he argues, Foucault has been misunderstood as saying 'that thoughts, things, etc., are in fact produced by language', whereas of course, for Hunter, and for us, 'discourse is not a particularly linguistic phenomenon' (Hunter n.d.). He goes so far as to suggest we might not want to use the term at all. Obviously we do not want to go this far (obvious because we are in the middle of this long discussion introducing you to a way of handling the term), although we think it is a sound enough suggestion. Instead, we want further to clarify what a non-linguistic notion of discourse looks like in action, to offer you more hints about how you might use this notion in your work.

The non-discursive

One point remains before we lay out some steps for using our reworked notion of discourse, and this concerns the troublesome idea of the non-discursive. As we said above, Foucault's work does not suggest that everything is discourse. Our earlier example concerned sex and sexuality, and here we discuss the related example of the body. Bodies are not discourse, they are non-discursive in their materiality. But bodies do not exist and operate in a non-discursive vacuum. Of course the word 'body' is itself a discursive production, but more than this, the entity that is the body is under the sovereignty of discourse (in *Birth of the Clinic* Foucault [1973] talks about psychopathology as the 'form of specification' of the body).

Even if we think of an extreme body practice like torture, we are within the ambit of a discursive practice. Torture is discursive inasmuch as it is always-already inscribed in a series of statements. Under the influence of the Foucaultian way of thinking, we can go so far as to say that this discursive sovereignty changes the material, in this case the body. Of course this is not to say that statements directly change bodies under torture. Rather, to draw on some work on torture by Peters (1985) and by Williams (1993), torture works on bodies directed by discourses, particularly discourses of law and ethics. In this way, Greek and Roman law, basing their practices on current ethical conceptions of personhood and honour, prohibited the testimony of slaves *except* under pain of torture (the thinking was that slaves were not ethically fully formed in the way citizens were, and lacked a commitment to honour to the extent that their testimony could only be relied on if it were extracted from them under torture). The bodies of the slaves were not directly attacked by the statements of ethics and law, yet these statements oversaw the direct attack which was the torture, to the point where it would be most unwise to try to understand the non-discursive bodies independently of the discursive field. The body's form is not independent of discourse, and articulations of the body (in a wide sense) are always discursive, yet the body itself is non-discursive.

'Hold on,' you might reasonably say at this point, 'surely there are some non-discursive things which are completely outside the influence of any discourse. What about the natural world?' Well, there may still be a problem here. Our argument is that no objects exist in a completely non-discursive realm, so we should take a little time to demonstrate that 'nature' is best handled in the way we handled bodies. It would be most unwise to try to understand non-discursive nature independently of the discourses of nature. We are immediately aided in this by the work of Bruno Latour, whom we meet on more intimate terms in the next chapter. In his *Science in Action* (1987: 94–100), Latour argues that 'nature' can never be the final arbiter about any dispute in science: other forms of justification are constantly needed because of arguments about 'the composition, content, expression and meaning of that [nature's] voice'. Nature is only ever a *post hoc* justification of an established fact. In other words, Latour is arguing that the 'facts' of natural phenomena follow discourse, not the other way around: they enter into discourse as produced 'truths'. So, to take an example of a supposedly natural phenomenon, to us rain is a precipitation derived from clouds. Let's suppose that there were a group of ancient thinkers for whom rain was the urine of the gods. This would suggest that rain has a changing discursive existence, that there is no point searching for a completely non-discursive object 'rain'. While we moderns might like to think science can provide us with just such an object 'rain', this object 'rain as precipitation from clouds' is only guaranteed through scientific theory – but the problem is that science is a discourse like any other, and we have no way of measuring the productions of one discourse ('science') against another ('religion').

If your objection goes so far as to ask at this point the questions, 'How does one examine scientific theory?' and 'What is the relation between science and the materiality that science takes as its object?', Foucault has an answer for you too. Such questions can only be asked because scientific discourse has already made the objects of science visible. This is not an alternative route to a pure pre-discursive realm of existence. These visibilities are not reflections of the pure forms of objects, but rather the result of temporary discursive luminosity; they allow a thing to exist only as a flash, sparkle or shimmer. As Deleuze comments, discussing Foucault's *The Birth of the Clinic*, 'each historical medical formation modulated a first light and constituted a space of visibility for illness, making symptoms gleam' (1986: 58).

It's worth pointing out that Ian Hacking has a slightly different take on this problem, which may be more to your taste. Hacking (1992a) suggests that there are indeed natural objects in the world that exist independently of human discourse. However, he runs the line that when one investigates areas like mental illness, it is apparent that these categories do not exist independently of the definitional work of those who 'make up' the area. Latour and Hacking are not so far apart as you might imagine here: Latour is not, we suggest, making the rather anthropocentric claim that nothing exists in nature unless it is part of human discourse; rather, he is seeking to demonstrate the logical impossibility of demonstrating nature as a priori. If you are keen to get your teeth into this controversy, have a look at Hacking's (1992a) account of the invention of multiple personality disorder (since renamed 'dissociative identity disorder').

One final point of clarification is necessary before we push on to offer the 'steps to take in using the Foucaultian notion of discourse' we promised earlier. While we stress that discourses are not closed systems – the possibility of innovation in discourse is always present within any discourse itself and within tangential or succeeding discourses – we acknowledge that some discursive formations behave as closed and are sometimes treated in this way. For example, much of Jacques Derrida's work suggests that metaphysics attempts to maintain a closed status and thus attempts to blind us to other possibilities. We can only urge you to be wary of such 'closures'; a thorough-going Foucaultian approach to discourse will always allow you to see possibilities of innovation.

Steps to take in using the Foucaultian notion of discourse

Julian Henriques and his co-authors provide an excellent building block:

> [Discourse] is regulated and systematic. An important proposition is related to this recognition: the rules are not confined to those internal to the discourse, but include rules of combination with other discourses, rules that establish differences from other categories of discourse (for example scientific as opposed to literary, etc.), the rules of production of the possible statements. The rules delimit the sayable. But (except for axiomatic systems such as chess) they do not imply a closure. The systematic character of a discourse includes its systematic articulation with other discourses. In practice, discourses delimit what can be said, while providing the spaces – the concepts, metaphors, models, analogies, for making new statements within any specific discourse. . . . The analysis which we propose regards every discourse as the result of a practice of production which is at once material, discursive and complex, always inscribed in relation to other practices of production of discourse. Every discourse is part of a discursive complex; it is locked in an intricate web of practices, bearing in mind that every practice is by definition both discursive and material. (1984: 105–6)

We can extract from this passage a 'simple' set of five steps for using the Foucaultian notion of discourse. We mark the word 'simple' in this way because we can't quite leave it there – it would be misleading to say 'simple' steps are all that is involved with this notion; from what we've said about discourse so far you already know some elaboration is necessary. What we can do is keep the steps themselves as simple as possible and, after presenting them in simple form, elaborate each one briefly by relating it to our more complex discussion of discourse up to this point.

The starting step to glean from the above passage is:

1   the recognition of a discourse as a corpus of 'statements' whose organisation is regular and systematic.

The subsequent steps cannot be taken until this one has been safely negotiated, for they relate to the fact that in being regular and systematic discourses have rules. These remaining four steps are steps of rule identification. They are:

2   the identification of rules of the production of statements;
3   the identification of rules that delimit the sayable (which of course are never rules of closure);
4   the identification of rules that create the spaces in which new statements can be made;
5   the identification of rules that ensure that a practice is material and discursive at the same time.

Each of these five steps, we stress before launching into our elaboration of them, can be followed whether you are analysing a discourse in isolation, that is, considering the rules internal to it, or the operation of a cluster of discourses, that is, considering the rules of combination as well as those internal to individual discourses.

It is not too difficult to elaborate Step 1 – recognising a discourse as a corpus of 'statements' whose organisation is regular and systematic – for this is the basic step we had to take you through to say anything at all about the Foucaultian way of treating the notion of discourse. It's almost as if you could not be reading this chapter sensibly without having taken this step (if it's all gobbledygook to you still, then we've failed to take you through even this first step; we'll push on assuming you're not in this camp). Perhaps the point in the preceding discussion at which Step 1 is most clear is the point at which we first alerted you to the danger of confusing the term 'discourse' with 'language'. To make any sense of this point you must know that there is at least something 'regular and systematic' about each of these terms; if you didn't, you would have no way of ever hoping to regularly and systematically distinguish them one from the other. Of course this doesn't mean that you can necessarily recognise discourse as a set of regular and systematic 'statements', in the somewhat peculiar Foucaultian use of this term. For this you need also to know that statements involve 'things' as well as 'words'. Probably the clearest expression of this aspect of this step is the example Curtly expounded for us, about industrial law discourse. You might just like to pause at this stage and see if you can think of some other 'discourses' (medicine, psychology, etc.) which would be fair game for the next four steps.

When Curtly lets us know that we cannot go beyond the discursive surface of industrial law to a 'deeper outside' of industrial 'things', that these industrial 'things' have no independent existence in a realm to which industrial law must defer, he is implicitly also telling us that the discourse of industrial law is always made up of statements that encapsulate both industrial 'words' and industrial 'things'. And when he tells us that these 'words' and 'things' are the result of the operation of a public apparatus of law, he is also telling us that the discourse of industrial law, like other legal discourses, is recognisable as 'law' precisely because these statements are regular and systematic. If this were not the case, 'law' would be indistinguishable from other discourses.

In elaborating Step 2 – the identification of rules of the production of statements – we first return to the example of sexuality we situated at the beginning of our discussion of discourse. To say that sexuality only emerged from the eighteenth century is to say that this discourse has only been in production since then. This is, in turn, to invite examination of the rules by which the statements which make up this discourse were and are produced – the shifts in thinking about sex alluded to earlier, and so on. The points we made, using Hunter, about Foucault fragmenting 'thinking' and 'reference' also fit here. In urging us to forget the idea of a thinking process prior to the use of words and symbols and to move away from the idea of a fixed point of reference for all words and symbols, Foucault is also urging us to concentrate on the rules of the production of different statements. Earlier we borrowed Hunter's examples of a simple mathematical discourse and the more complex discourse of confession and we invented two examples of our own, one through Steffi, concerned with student political discourse, and the other, through Curtly, the just-discussed example of industrial law discourse. In this context we suggest that these examples will also allow you to highlight the public aspects – schooling, church rituals, the operation of a variety of student political mechanisms and the operation of a variety of legal mechanisms, respectively – of the rules of the production of statements in these four discourses. We also pointed out that this is a subjectless process – that the rules of the production of statements are not centred on human intervention or action.

The third and fourth steps in our guide to using the Foucaultian notion of discourse – the identification of rules that delimit the sayable (which are never rules of closure) and the identification of rules that create the spaces in which new statements can be made – cover similar ground to Step 2. In identifying the rules by which statements are produced, we are in one sense already identifying the rules that delimit the sayable and the rules by which new statements are made. Therefore in elaborating Steps 3 and 4 we need to pay close attention to those features which will allow you to differentiate them from Step 2.

In regard to limiting the sayable, we can also use the example of sexuality from the beginning of our discussion of discourse. In saying that this discourse has only been in production since the eighteenth century and hence drawing attention to the rules by which the statements which make up this discourse were and are produced, we are also drawing attention to the rules which limit what can be said about sexuality. For example, the rules by which 'scientific' psychiatric statements about sexuality are produced disallow statements based on magic and witchcraft, statements that would have been sayable under a discourse based on 'the flesh'. The points from Hunter about Foucault fragmenting 'thinking' and 'reference' are relevant again here. In urging us to concentrate on the rules of the production of different statements rather than seeking the origins of thought, Foucault is including a focus on limits as a part of the focus on production. Hunter's examples of a simple mathematical discourse and the more complex discourse of confession can each be offered with an eye to the limits of the sayable as much as to the conditions of production.

The only extra point required by way of elaboration of this step is the point we made about closure. We confessed a certain impotence about the problem of closure earlier – urging you to be wary of discourses which appear closed – and we are equally lame here. The problem for us (and of course we're handing it on to you like a hot potato) is that the sort of discourses we mentioned earlier (we borrowed Derrida's example of metaphysical discourses; some religious discourses and some scientific discourses are also good examples) have built their capacity to appear closed over a long time. When we say you should maintain the possibility of innovation at all times, we admit that it would be quite reasonable for you to fire back an 'Easier said than done'. Indeed it is; holding open the possibility of innovation in the face of a discourse that presents a 'We've had things wrapped up for a long time' face to the world is a daunting prospect. Our lame addition here is to reiterate that you will undoubtedly increase your capacity for recognising the openness of all discourses the more you practise the philosophical scepticism we outlined in the previous chapter.

In regard to Step 4 – identifying the rules by which new statements are made – yet again we can use the example of sexuality and Hunter's examples of mathematics and 'sins of the flesh'. In discussing the rules by which the statements which make up each of these discourses were and are produced, we are also, almost tautologically, discussing the rules by which new statements are made. The other points of elaboration necessary in regard to this step help us better differentiate this step from Step 2, to rid ourselves of the spectre of tautology. This step concentrates more on the novelty of new statements – their *newness* – where the other step concentrates on their production. It is through this step, then, that you will be able to most satisfactorily present the inventiveness of discourses, the way they invent new forms of person, like the mentally ill and the criminal, and the way they invent new categories for understanding human nature, like sexuality. In doing so, you will also be able to highlight the fact that this inventiveness is based on quite public apparatuses like schools, hospitals and prisons, not on some private operations of 'great minds'. This inventiveness does not reduce to anything – it is not amenable to being encapsulated in some or other 'essence'. Moreover, you will even be able to give sensible Foucaultian answers to the particular questions which the novelty aspects of discourses of science always seem to raise. You will be able at least to address, if not completely dispel, some of the intellectual myths which surround scientific production by breaking the newness of scientific statements down into sets of thoughts and practices (what Latour calls 'networks').

Our elaboration of Step 5 – the identification of rules that ensure that a practice is material and discursive at the same time – returns us particularly to our exposition of Foucault's handling of the idea of the non-discursive, but to much else besides. At almost every point in our discussion of the Foucaultian approach to discourse lurks the anti-Hegelian (and hence anti-Marxist) theme of the inseparability of materiality and thought. Where Hegel and Marx concern themselves with the proper relation of the material and the ideational, Foucault expounds the decidedly sceptical line that intellectual inquiry is much more fruitfully directed at the ways objects refuse this distinction. The rules involved here ensure that, for instance, prison practices are always about discourses like penology, or their precursors or successors, *and* the materiality of prison structures and prison life, that sexual practices are always about discourses like sexology, psychology, or their precursors or successors, *and* the materiality of sex. These rules also ensure that knowledge cannot be reduced to thinking, thoughts, opinions, ideas, and so on, but is best understood as a material practice with definite, public, material conditions of operation like literacy training, schooling more generally, printing, professional organisations for only some knowledge endeavours (the sciences, engineering, medicine, etc.), and many others. The rules of this step allow Steffi to recognise that her student political activity is best viewed as a combination of discourse and materiality rather than as straight 'action', as many of her friends believe, and they allow Curtly – at last – to be more patient in dealing with industrial law, to see it as a complex mix of discourses and material practices, not as a site of material action distinguishable from non-material thinking about it. These rules also help us stop ourselves from searching for 'deeper' reality behind or beneath discourses.

In regard to the notion of the non-discursive, this step might appear to you contradictory. 'How can you say, on the one hand,' you might sensibly ask of us, somewhat exasperated, 'that we are meant to identify rules that ensure that a practice is material and discursive at the same time, when you earlier told us, on the other, that, for example, bodies are non-discursive in their materiality?' It's a good question when phrased like this, though it suggests that you are forgetting the point we made immediately after telling you that bodies are non-discursive in their materiality – that bodies do not exist and operate in a non-discursive vacuum. It is this idea of the perpetually pervasive influence of discourse that allows us to resolve the apparent contradiction. For us, and we hope for you too, there is ultimately no contradiction.

The rules that ensure practices are material and discursive at the same time do not rule out the possibility of non-discursivity, but they do ensure that the non-discursive is always within the ambit of discourse, under its sovereignty. Our earlier example of tortured bodies demonstrates this point well. In examining practices of torture we can identify rules by which these practices are always, for us, material *and* discursive (about inflicting torment on actual bodies under the influence of discourses like those of Greek and Roman law that categorise slaves in a particular way), yet these rules still allow us to understand the bodies at the centre of these practices as non-discursive. While nothing is completely non-discursive, not even 'obvious' candidates like 'nature', this does not wipe the idea of non-discursivity from our intellectual plate.

At last, we've said all we have to say about the Foucaultian way of handling the notion of discourse (and not before time you might think). Now it's your turn.

EXERCISE 2.4

Making use of our full discussion on discourse, but focusing on the five steps we laid out – (1) the recognition of a discourse as a corpus of 'statements' whose organisation is regular and systematic; (2) the identification of rules of the production of statements; (3) the identification of rules that delimit the sayable (which of course are never rules of closure); (4) the identification of rules that create the spaces in which new statements can be made; (5) the identification of rules that ensure that a practice is material and discursive at the same time – write a paragraph or two on the way each step might be taken in analysing the following account of Luther's role in the process by which Protestant interpretations of the notion of the calling developed towards the spirit of capitalism, an account largely borrowed, obviously, from Max Weber's famous *The Protestant Ethic and the Spirit of Capitalism* (1989).

Weber discusses the religious roots of Luther's very traditionalistic understanding of a calling. 'Luther read the Bible through the spectacles of his whole attitude . . . from about 1518 to 1530 this not only remained traditionalistic but became ever more so.' Luther's traditionalism was at first a matter of Pauline indifference – 'One may attain salvation in any walk of life; on the short pilgrimage of life there is no use in laying weight on the form of occupation' – but as he personally became more involved in worldly affairs, he came to place more value on work in the world, but as a matter of Divine Will, a matter of Providence, not in any way as a precursor of a spirit of capitalism. Because this belief in Providence identified 'absolute obedience to God's will . . . with absolute acceptance of things as they were . . . it was impossible for Luther to establish a new or in any way fundamental connection between worldly activity and religious principles'. Luther's 'calling is something which man has to accept as a divine ordinance, to which he must adapt himself'. It did not embrace the idea that work in the calling is '*the* . . . task set by God'. Orthodox Lutheranism reinforced this, producing a negative ethics whereby 'obedience to authority and acceptance of things as they were, were preached'. Luther 'could not but suspect the tendency of ascetic self-discipline of leading to salvation by works, and hence he and his Church were forced to keep it more and more in the background'.

Weber concludes that Luther's idea of the calling is of only very small importance for his, Weber's, study. He directs our attention instead to other forms of Protestantism 'in which a relation between practical life and religious motivation can be more easily perceived' (Weber 1989: 84–7, emphasis in original).

One other task may also keep you amused: as you write your paragraphs, you might also like to think about the way Weber's approach can be characterised as 'total history' while your understanding of discourse of course pushes you in the direction of a 'general history'.

Power

Power–knowledge

Weeks had passed since Curtly's very dark day in class. Feeling a little more confident after having worked his way through archaeology, genealogy and discourse, during another discussion about Foucault, he suddenly blurted out, 'Yes, it's all about power.'

He regretted it immediately. His interlocutors from the 'dark day' were ready to pounce. 'Come on Curtly, that's just another wild generalisation.'

Curtly's hackles began to rise, but then a strange feeling (strange for Curtly anyway) came over him and he found himself agreeing with his detractors. 'You're right,' he said with perfect deference, 'archaeology, genealogy, and discourse rely on the nexus Foucault sees between power and knowledge, but this doesn't mean they are all *about power.'*

Wow, Curtly is learning the caution we've seen only in Steffi so far. It remains for us to spell out some of the details of the intricate relationship between power and knowledge to which Curtly referred. It is this relationship, as he indicated, that allows Foucault and Foucaultians to keep their (and others') heads from spinning as they employ the tools of archaeology, genealogy and discourse as techniques in the distinctively Foucaultian approach to history.

We could at this point launch into a diatribe about what Foucault means by power, but this would take a book in itself. For our purposes we need only a partial exploration of the Foucaultian notion of power, enough to tie it carefully to knowledge, an exploration of how it forms the power–knowledge nexus that renders the Foucaultian approach to history unique, and in so doing the way it informs the Foucaultian use of archaeology, genealogy and discourse. We can start at a spot we recently visited – the relation between the discursive and the non-discursive.

This is, as we have already discussed, a discursive relation. That is to say, in the relationship between the discursive and the non-discursive, Foucault accords a primary role to the former. In this way, the field of knowledge can be said to be dominated by the primacy of discourse. However, we can be more specific about discursive relations by adding that they are relations of power. Power relations serve to make the connections, discussed earlier, between the visible and the sayable (the two poles of knowledge), yet they exist outside these poles. In other words, to help you out of what's looking like a trap of circularity, while discourse dominates knowledge, it is not possible to talk of a discourse–knowledge nexus if we are to remain Foucaultians. It is not possible because Foucault puts so much effort into separating this aspect of discursive relations from others and treating it as a separate concept, a concept he refers to by the term 'power'.

In many ways this choice of term is a fairly unhappy one, at least in English. As we've seen with other terms that enjoy some prominence in the world of Foucaultian scholarship, it too easily has become all things to all people. More than that, it has taken on a most unfortunate association with conspiracy thinking, such that to many people who employ the term, 'power' is always something hidden in the background doing dirty work (obviously there's a connection here with the 'hidden meaning' syndrome we discussed earlier in regard to Marxism). As we'll see shortly, Foucault doesn't mean this at all. It's probably wise, as we head into a discussion of how Foucault sorts power out as a separate aspect of discursive relations, particularly in association with knowledge, that you bear in mind the much more mundane use of the term 'power' in English, describing energy sources. In gritting your teeth and getting along with yet another troublesome term, remembering this more mundane usage might prove beneficial. As Hunt and Wickham put it:

> 'Power' is a technical term involved in the always-incomplete operation of a machine. Just as the term 'power' is commonly used to refer to the technical process by which petrol fuels an incomplete (imperfect) internal combustion

engine for it to (imperfectly) drive a car, or the technical process by which coal, water or nuclear fission fuels an incomplete (imperfect) electricity grid to (imperfectly) drive any number of electrical appliances, so, we suggest, we should think of power in society. Engines drive cars and electricity drives appliances 'incompletely' or 'imperfectly' in the sense that they do not operate completely or perfectly, they are not expected to operate perpetually in exactly the same way, something always goes wrong. The only perpetual aspect of the process is the perpetual process of keeping the process going. ... In these examples power is the process of 'keeping things going', it is not a 'thing', in the way fuel or electricity is. (1994: 80–1)

Another way to help make this point about the distinctiveness of what Foucault means by 'power' involves a brief examination of some Marxists' reaction to what he has to say. It is interesting that Foucault's work on power should have attracted so much interest among Marxists, though usually as something to name-check and then ignore. Foucault is used to establish modernness, authenticity, scholarship, but little is actually *done* with Foucault's work on power. For example, Stuart Hall (1988a: 3) agrees with Foucault that '[p]ower is never merely repressive but, in Foucault's sense, always productive', but then carries on to write a text about political power which does not make use of this insight: political power is conceptualised as the possession of politicians and other figures. Similarly, Rosalind Brunt (1989) makes a show of acknowledging the value of Foucault's work on power, but then immediately returns to a 'conspiracy' theory of power, whereby powerful people oppress the masses; she talks of '"regimes" of power, exercised by knowledge-holders like doctors and priests, whose expertise grants authority and legitimates their active hold over those who lack the knowledge'. Laclau and Mouffe (1985: 152), likewise, 'can affirm, with Foucault, that wherever there is power there is resistance', but still concern themselves with class struggle and subordination (themes pointedly avoided by Foucault) in an attempt to develop their own kind of 'Gramscianism'. Furthermore, Duccio Trombadori, an interlocutor of Foucault's, is worried about the disappearance of 'real' subjects in Foucault – that is, about the disappearance of materiality in Foucault's work – and the lack of any account of who struggles against whom: 'One profound criticism [of Foucault] remains that of the lack of individuating real *subjects* who are capable of determining a relation of power ... *who* struggles against *whom*?' (in Foucault 1991: 112–13, emphasis in original).

Let's do a little more than pay lip-service to Foucault on power. In fact, let's start by forgetting about 'politics' for the time being. To return to Foucault's philosophical formulations, we can say that power is a *strategy*, a strategy that maintains a relation between the sayable and the visible. The visible is always in danger of exhaustion because it is completely determined by the sayable; the problem is one of how visibilities, being completely receptive, in contrast to the spontaneity of the sayable, are inexhaustible. This is something of a recurrent problem in philosophy. For example, for Kant, understanding was a determining element over intuition and thus the problem arose of the inexhaustibleness of intuition; Kant's solution was the 'mysterious imagination'. For Foucault, the solution lies in regarding the two poles of knowledge as always in conflict, and he is fond of describing their inter-relation by martial metaphors. The sayable and the visible are divided from each other, yet insinuate themselves inside the relation between the other and its conditions. The sayable offers the visible in a 'space of dissemination', while offering itself up as a 'form of exteriority' (Deleuze 1986: 66, 73). Consequently, in the conduct of an archaeology, for example, one reveals something of the visible in opening up statements, and something of the statement in opening up visibilities. As we said earlier, in his *Discipline and Punish* (1977), Foucault shows how the prison as a form of visibility produces statements which reintroduce criminality, while statements around criminality produce forms of visibility which reinforce prison. There is, then, a necessary double relation between the two forms that is *productive* – and this is one of the features of Foucaultian methods: power is productive, and this is what Foucault means when he says power is positive not negative.

The notion of the contest within this double relation is not sufficient, however, because the primacy of the sayable suggests it can be the only victor; hence the need to introduce a more complex understanding of power. Foucault's account of power, then, is, at least in part, an account of the ways the visible is not overcome by the sayable, as first appearances would suggest.

Deleuze summarises Foucault's treatment of power (using quotations from Foucault's [1982] 'The Subject and Power') in the following terms:

> Power is a relation between forces, or rather every relation between forces is a power relation. . . . Force is never singular but essentially exists in relation with other forces, such that any force is already a relation, that is to say power: force has no other subject or object than force. . . . It is 'an action upon an action, on existing actions, or on those which may arise in the present or in the future'; it is 'a set of actions upon other actions'. We can therefore conceive of a necessarily open list of variables expressing a relation between forces or power relation, constituting actions upon actions: to incite, to induce, to seduce, to make easy or difficult, to enlarge or limit, to make more or less probable, and so on. (1986: 70)

Power, then, is not essentially repressive; it is not possessed, but is practised. Power is not the prerogative of 'masters', but passes through every force. We should think of power not as an attribute (and ask 'What is it?'), but as an exercise (and ask 'How does it work?').

In addition, forces have a capacity for resistance, such that power is only exercised in relation to a resistance, each force having the power to affect and be affected by other forces. We cannot emphasise this point strongly enough. For Foucault, resistance to power is part of the exercise of power (part of how it works). As Hunt and Wickham argue, after discussing politics in terms of contestation:

Resistance is a technical component of governance, a component heavily involved in the fact that governance is always subject to politics. Resistance is part of the fact that power can only ever make a social machinery run imperfectly or incompletely. . . . In Foucault's words, resistance is the 'counter-stroke' to power, a metaphor with strong technical, machine-like connotations. Power and resistance are together the governance machine of society, but only in the sense that together they contribute to the truism that 'things never quite work', not in the conspiratorial sense that resistance serves to make power work perfectly. (1994: 83)

Resistance, then, is not a source of despair or celebration. The task of analysts, such as you and us, is to describe the way in which resistance operates as a part of power, not to seek to promote or oppose it.

Thus far we have established power as a series of relations between forces, and knowledge as a series of relations between forms. The question remains: what are the relations between these relations, what are the relations between power and knowledge? The two are completely heterogeneous, but engage in a process of contest with one another similar to that we saw operating between the forms of knowledge. However, power passes through forces not forms; it is diagrammatic (Foucault discusses the Panopticon as diagram in *Discipline and Punish* [1977: 205] in the following terms: the presentation of the relations between forces unique to a particular formation; the distribution of the power to affect and be affected; the mixing of non-formalised pure functions and unformed pure matter; a transmission or distribution of particular features). In being diagrammatic in this way, power mobilises non-stratified matter and functions, it is local and unstable, and is flexible. Knowledge is stratified, archivised and rigidly segmented. Power is strategic, but it is anonymous. The strategies of power are mute and blind, precisely because they *avoid* the forms of knowledge, the sayable and the visible.

Foucault characterises the workings of power as 'microphysical' (the term 'microphysics' is intended by Foucault to distinguish himself from Kant: Kant's practical determination is irreducible to a *connaissance*, or knowledge of a thing, whereas Foucault is concerned that the practice of power be irreducible to a *savoir*, or knowing how to do something). This should be taken not as referring to a miniaturisation, but rather as a characterisation of power as mobile and localisable. Power and knowledge are mutually dependent and exist in a relation of interiority to each other, although Foucault accords power a kind of primacy: power would exist (although only in a virtual form) without knowledge, whereas knowledge would have nothing to integrate without differential power relations.

Perhaps this point is easier to see if we put it more bluntly, if we consider the role of knowledge in actually supporting certain techniques of power, if we ask 'How?', not 'Why?' Remembering that Hunt and Wickham refer to techniques of power by the term 'governance', we can usefully borrow from them again:

> Knowledge is involved in . . . attempts to impose more control or management:
> the economy should be slowed, the economy should be stimulated; the war
> should be stepped up, the war should be ended. . . . Here knowledge is being
> used to select some techniques of [power] over others and to implement the
> chosen techniques in the attempts to impose control or management on the
> objects concerned. . . . The knowledge used ranges from very simple, informal
> knowledge to very complex, formal knowledge and the range includes know-
> ledge called rational, within modern social sciences, and knowledge called
> irrational. . . . Even the governance of an economy . . . involves techniques which
> combine knowledge in a similar way. Monetarist techniques for governing
> inflation, for instance, are informed by a combination of: complex, formal (very
> rational) knowledge based on economic theories and models designed to deter-
> mine the effects of changes in the money supply on economic well-being which
> is passed on in formal government documents, journal articles and newspapers;
> simple, informal knowledge to do with which policies are likely to find favour
> with government officials or international bankers which is passed on in infor-
> mal conversations in hallways and tea-rooms; and, in addition, not a little blind
> faith that this is 'how people really are' (sometimes called voodoo economics).
> (1994: 90)

Hunt and Wickham offer the following elaboration:

> Three closely connected points need to be stressed in the light of Foucault's
> direct influence. First, the knowledge which is used in the actual governing of
> objects is always available knowledge. We stress 'available' because Foucault
> elaborates the ways some knowledge is made available by the operations of the
> institutions involved in instances of governance while other knowledge is not
> made available. It is in elaborating the complex relations between definite insti-
> tutions and available knowledge that Foucault's generalisations about the con-
> nections between . . . [power] and knowledge are best seen. . . . Second,
> Foucault's work details the rise of those formal knowledge complexes known as
> the human sciences and traces many of the ways they have come to inform
> widely used techniques of . . . [power] in the modern world: new knowledge of
> madness generated by psychiatry being used in the governance of deviance;
> new knowledge of punishment generated by penology. . . . Third, Foucault indi-
> cates, an indication taken up strongly by some of his followers (Hacking 1975,
> 1990; Rose 1991; Miller and Rose 1990), the importance of statistical knowledge
> for many modern techniques of . . . [power]. This point is especially relevant to
> the government of modern nation states. (1994: 91)

Power and subjects

Another crucial aspect of power, and one implicated in the power–knowledge nexus, concerns subjectivity. This is crucial because in Foucault's
account of power the formation of subjects is part and parcel of power's
productivity. Foucault writes: 'My objective . . . has been to create a history
of the different modes by which, in our culture, human beings are made
subjects' (1982: 208). Foucault is proposing the subject not as producer, but
as product:

One has to dispense with the constituent subject, to get rid of the subject itself, that's to say, to arrive at an analysis which can account for the constitution of the subject within a historical framework. (1980c: 117)

This is not to say that Foucault disavows an active role for subjects; far from it. Subjects are active in producing themselves. More than that, they are active in producing themselves as subjects in the sense of *subjected* to power: 'An immense labor to which the West has submitted generations in order to produce . . . men's subjection: their constitution as subjects in both senses of the word' (1978b: 60).

The term 'subjectivity' (a somewhat simplified translation of the multiple meanings of the French *asujetissement*) is used by us to mark a difference from the more usual term 'individual'. The individual is usually understood as a rational being, the origin of human action, forming a unitary and non-contradictory object occupying the same physical space as the body. Yet for Foucaultians, of course, this 'individual' is an historically contingent phenomenon, an invention only rigorously defined in the nineteenth century (on the birth of the psychological individual, see Venn 1984; Rose 1985). In choosing to problematise this figure of the individual, partly by using the term 'subject' or 'subjectivity', Foucaultians seek to explain how this emerging psychological invention came to be seen as the 'site' where sexuality, and so on, take place, and how it becomes an object of 'technologies of the self'. (This term was actually developed by Foucault well after the publication of *The Archaeology of Knowledge* to describe the processes of construction of selfhood through the workings of psychological and other formal knowledge groupings, or sciences. These knowledge groupings are 'technological' in the sense that they are systematic mini- or inter-discourses implicated in self-construction. The etymology of 'technology', from the Greek *techne*, implies an art or skill, particularly a constructive skill, so 'technology' in its Foucaultian sense is precisely such a 'construction' or production.)

As with so many other Foucaultian formulations, the notion of discourse is involved again here. Subjects' actions take place in discourse, and subjects themselves are produced through discourse. Subjects are the punctuation of discourse, and provide the bodies on and through which discourse may act. In line with this we may say that subjects form some of the conditions for knowledge. For Foucault, the subject is produced out of the doubling of force upon itself, the attention to self. This production of subjectivity always occurs as a doubling of self upon self in every realm – in the realm of the body, the realm of force and the realm of knowledge. Human action within discourse is always positional, that is, it always occurs through a subject position inhabiting a space between the two poles of knowledge, the discursive and the non-discursive.

Such a treatment of the subject, while distinct from standard, psychological treatments of 'the individual', has important repercussions for this figure. Theoretically, we need no longer depend (should we so choose) on 'the individual' as the origin of all things. Rather than think of the single figure 'individual' in different sites, we can think of different subject positions taken up in discourse, positions that can be and are contradictory and irrational. For a Foucaultian account of the subject, attention must be drawn to the ways in which power relations differentially position subjects in discourse, even when (perhaps especially when) this produces 'contradictory subjectivity'.

It might be thought that such an account of the subject raises the problems of discourse determinism and the essentialisation of power: the subject seems at times to be moved mechanically through discourse by the workings of power relations which themselves only seem to be exercised through what we might term a 'will to power'. Against this possibility, we argue that the complex intertwining of power, knowledge and the subject precludes the questions of origin and of determination. For us, the triad power, knowledge and the subject is so systematic that it makes little sense to consider each component separately – they all condition, and form the conditions for, each other. Thus it is inaccurate to suggest that discourse determines the subject, or that power *in the last instance* is responsible for the production of subjectivity: the circularity of interdependence precludes questions of primacy, since none of the components of the triad would exist (except in a virtual form) without the others.

Once again, it is your turn to write – this time, about power.

EXERCISE 2.5

Please select any published Foucaultian account of power–knowledge at work (you may choose one cited in this chapter or you may prefer to select one from elsewhere – it may focus on a school, a prison, a hospital, or whatever) and then write a brief essay (about 1,000 words) discussing the way at least four of the following summary points about power–knowledge are used (or not used) in it.

- Power–knowledge helps in the use of the tools of archaeology, genealogy and discourse, allowing their use to be part of the distinctive Foucaultian approach to history.
- Our limited account of Foucault's understanding of power starts with discourse – discursive relations are power relations, connecting the visible and the sayable, but we cannot talk of discourse–knowledge if we are to remain Foucaultians as Foucault put so much effort into separating power from other aspects of discourse.
- 'Power' is something of a problematic term, partly because it has too often become associated with conspiracy thinking. One way to help overcome this problem is to think of power in technical terms and to remember that the term itself has some mundane uses to do with things working.

- Foucault's approach to power is quite different to Marxist approaches, even where Marxists try to use Foucault's work to make their points.
- Power is a strategy concerned with relations between the visible and the sayable, preventing the exhaustion of the visible. Foucault regards these two elements of power as always in conflict. The sayable and the visible are divided from each other, yet insinuate themselves inside the relation between the other and its conditions. This necessary double relation between the two forms is productive. Hence, for Foucault, power is productive; this is what he means when he says power is positive not negative.
- Power is not repressive or possessed, but practised.
- Resistance to power is crucial, but it should be neither celebrated nor feared. It is a technical component of power, part of its operation.
- While power is a relation of forces and knowledge is a relation of forms, the two relate to each other as different but complementary. Power is non-stratified, local, unstable and flexible; knowledge is stratified, stable and segmented. Power actually *avoids* the forms of knowledge. Do not make the mistake of thinking power and knowledge are the same thing, which is one vulgar reading of Foucault. As Foucault himself remarked, if they were simply the same thing it would have been a waste of most of his scholarly life to analyse their relation!
- In seeing power as 'microphysical' – mobile and localisable – Foucault positions it in the relationship with knowledge as having a slight primacy – power would exist, at least in some form, without knowledge, but knowledge could not exist without power.
- This can be put more crudely by saying that knowledge supports power in action (in governance).
- Subjectivity is crucial to Foucault's account of power and hence to his account of power–knowledge. In being productive, power produces subjects. While subjects are products, this does not mean they are not active; they are active in producing themselves, producing themselves as subjects in the sense of those subjected to power.
- For Foucaultians, subjects are not the same as individuals in the standard psychological sense of the word. Where this sense assumes the existence of individuals as 'natural' and inevitable, Foucaultians understand this category as historically contingent, as an object of study about which nothing should be assumed.
- In considering individuals in this way (as an invented category rather than a natural phenomenon), Foucaultian work sometimes talks about 'technologies of the self' – inventions by which the self is 'revealed' or modified.

- As power is involved in subjectivity via discourse, we can say that subjects form some of the conditions for knowledge. Such a position involves, again, the rejection of the individual as the origin of all things, in favour of the idea of different subject positions in discourse, positions that can be and are contradictory and irrational.
- While this might look like discourse determinism, we argue that the triad power/knowledge/subjectivity is never about the origins of any one of the constituent parts of the triad, or about the origin of anything else. The fact that the components of the triad must always be considered together means that no determinism is involved.

Part II

SCIENCE AND CULTURE AS IMPORTANT
OBJECTS OF ANALYSIS FOR THOSE USING
FOUCAULT'S METHODS

3

'Why has everybody started following scientists around?'

Introduction: extending our methodological scope beyond the historical

Iva was feeling bewildered and not a little depressed. Well, depressed is probably not quite the right word, but it's fair to say her mood was quite dark as she tried to deal with her bewilderment. She'd spent the better part of two years studying Foucault's writing and familiarising herself with recent Foucaultian work on the self and the soul, among other things. It had taken a good deal of encouragement from her friend Martina to convince her that she would not only be welcome at the Foucault reading group, but that her contributions would be valued.

'I wouldn't say it was an unmitigated disaster,' Martina offered by way of lame reassurance.

'I would,' Iva retorted, too distressed to notice that she might be hurting her dear friend's feelings. 'Not a word, not a single bloody word. I took aeons to steel myself for a chatty performance and then had nothing at all to say, not a sausage. Who or what is this bloody Latour anyway? I was stupid enough to think I knew

at least something about most of the recent Foucaultian writers and they spent the whole night talking about someone who sounds like a wine maker to me.'

'Apparently he is from that family,' Martina said without much conviction, 'I heard one of those other newcomers say so as we were coming out.' She knew this wasn't much consolation to Iva, but it did help lighten the atmosphere a tidge.

Iva giggled slightly as she playfully remembered aloud that Martina had been no noisier than she had been during the agonising three hours. She added, with just a hint of sarcasm, 'Well our big wine discovery helps us situate him as a top-flight intellectual. Okay, let's get serious. Let's make a list of words that stick in our mind from the big disaster.'

'Science,' they both said simultaneously and loudly and fell about laughing as the tension fell away.

Iva and Martina are onto something important here. How has a concern with things Foucaultian, especially things of a methodological nature, led, with seemingly little effort, to a consideration of science? This is our main concern in this chapter. We hope to show Iva and Martina how this has happened and in so doing we hope to show you too.

So far, we have suggested that the prime method for any researcher inspired by Foucault is an historical method. This is not the same thing as doing history. Foucault's problem-based approach differs from the period- or event-based approach taken by most historians. In setting up a different method, Foucault can be said to be engaging in the analysis of knowledge, but he can also be said to be simultaneously stretching the boundaries of what usually counts as knowledge.

Of course the analysis of *knowledge* has a very long history. In sociology, in particular, specialist sociologists of knowledge have long been concerned to show how bodies of thought (legal, aesthetic, moral, religious, political, philosophical, etc.) are linked to and/or influenced by social and cultural factors (such as race, class and gender). Traditionally, however, *science* has been exempt from this sort of treatment, and has been regarded as a special case. In the last ten years or so, a group of thinkers who owe a considerable debt to Foucault have established something of a tradition of using his methods in the study of the formation of scientific truth. Bruno Latour is at the forefront of this group. It is this group that has so suddenly jumped into Iva and Martina's Foucaultian world. In setting at least some of the contents of their stall before you, to see if it tempts your tastebuds, we have first to take you back in time, just a wee bit.

In doing so we stress that one of the main inspirations for Foucault's novel approach to the analysis of knowledge was a body of work on the history of science by Bachelard and Canguilhem (see especially Bachelard 1968, 1986; Canguilhem 1989, 1990, 1994). In other words, there is a fundamental connection between Foucault's methods and the philosophy of science, although Foucault himself did not venture into the latter territory. Like Foucault, those at the forefront of the new 'science studies' approach (most notably Latour) make use of a *problem-based* approach in tackling scientific knowledge questions. As with Foucault, the overarching concern is with a description of the conditions that allow certain sets of scientific knowledge to emerge. (Perhaps the clearest link between these two 'traditions' of the analysis of knowledge – Foucault's approach and the 'science studies' approach – is given in a recent book by John Law, *Organizing Modernity* [1994]. Law's focus is on the [usually precarious] maintenance of social order. He draws extensively on Foucault's notion of discourse, which he extends by asking questions that foreground the *relational materialism* [1994: 23] that would mark any successful account of social order. Briefly, Law's concern is to extend a sociology of knowledge beyond human actors. As he bluntly puts it, 'left to their own devices *human actions and words do not spread very far at all. . . .* Other materials, such as texts and technologies, surely form a crucial part of any ordering' [1994: 24, emphasis in original]). It is in this similarity of concerns that we can see the extension of Foucault's methods into the analysis of science.

The beginnings of the sociology of science

While some sociologists have suggested that the reception of science, its order of occurrence or direction, might be socially influenced, they have frequently left out of their analyses the content or form of science, seeing it as, in effect, super-sociological (the account in this section draws heavily on Mulkay 1979; Woolgar 1988). In this way, it was a commonplace for nineteenth-century sociological thinkers to omit scientific knowledge as an investigable phenomenon. After Durkheim, a sociology of science was possible, but it was a sociology of how and why science came to oust religion, not a sociology of scientific knowledge itself. Durkheim's thinking on the matter looked like this: there are cultural variations in people's conception of many 'basics' (for example, time and space); these conceptions are not completely arbitrary, but arise in relation to a 'real' objective world; religious thought, the result of small collectivities, is being slowly replaced by science, which furnishes true knowledge of the 'real' objective world; science removes the collective, culturally contingent elements from ideas. Therefore, sociology, in Durkheim's view, had no need to study scientific knowledge because science was, by definition, absolutely and objectively true (see, for example, Durkheim 1915).

Marx is another good example of a nineteenth-century thinker who thought science was a special case. For Marx, human actions take place on a natural stage. Their actions transform that stage. In the course of acting on the natural stage, the human being gains knowledge about it. This knowledge is formulated as a result of the interests and economic concerns of dominant social groups, and is used to support particular social relationships. Marx suggested that the growth of science was intimately connected to the growth of capitalism. Because science could serve the technical interests of the bourgeoisie, science was fostered and grew massively, especially in the nineteenth century:

> The bourgeoisie . . . has created more massive and more colossal forces than have all preceding generations. Subjection of Nature's forces to man, machinery, application of chemistry to industry and agriculture, steam navigation, electric telegraphs. (Marx and Engels 1965: 47)

Elsewhere, Marx is explicit that capitalism is the direct cause of 'the development of the natural sciences to their highest point' (Marx 1973: 409).

Marx considered that science, like capitalism itself, was originally a liberating force inasmuch as it set people free from superstition and religion. In his view science was later perverted and set to use for exploitative purposes. Science, by this view, is closely linked to social circumstances and its uses and developments can only be understood by understanding the complexities of social organisation. However, the *content* of science is another matter entirely: for Marx, this is sharply distinguished from the world of ideology (law, politics, aesthetics, philosophy, religion, etc.). Indeed, Marxists have frequently tried to make Marxism 'scientific' – that is, objective, true, factual (writers like Althusser or Bourdieu are worth visiting if you are interested in this type of Marxism). Science and scientists may be ideological, but the content of scientific knowledge itself is above suspicion. As Mulkay remarks, for Marxists, scientists' 'knowledge-claims within their precise research areas are non-ideological' (1979: 10).

Science, then, may be regarded as prone to social factors, but scientific knowledge itself has come to be regarded as a special case, a case which sociology really has no right to consider, because there is nothing to explain. This trend continued well into the twentieth century. Karl Mannheim, for example, a very famous sociologist of knowledge, understood the phenomena of the natural world as constant and static. By his view, we gradually increase our knowledge of this natural world, eliminating error as we merrily chuff along and coming upon more and more truths as a result. Science, for this perspective, progresses in a straight line. This picture of the natural world is contrasted with a very different picture of the world of culture, which is not timeless and static , and which cannot be investigated in the same scientific way. Mannheim is clear that science is, epistemologically speaking, a special case, and it is for this reason that it is a special sociological case (see, for example, Mannheim 1936, 1952).

This was an enormously influential perspective. Werner Stark is a good example of a thinker who took the bait, hook, line and sinker. He tells us that scientific knowledge is a qualitatively different thing from knowledge in other fields: in philosophy, politics, and so on, new meanings have to be created, while in science, they merely have to be discovered:

> [T]he astronomer merely attempts to *grasp* the data, the *pre-existent* data: he is entirely controlled by them . . . the scientist allows himself to be impressed by

the objective truth of reality, the man of culture expresses the values in which he believes. (Stark 1958: 167, emphasis in original)

Let's sum up what this early sociology of science suggests before pushing on with our background sketch:

- The natural world is real and objective. Observers do not affect its qualities. Science is the branch of knowledge which seeks to provide an accurate picture of that world.
- Although the natural world is undergoing a certain amount of change, there are underlying universal and permanent aspects. We can come to understand these and the laws which express them by unbiased, detached observation.
- Because science has evolved stringent techniques for the observation of phenomena and the formation of laws of the universe, we can be confident about the empirical evidence gathered by scientists to help us put those laws of science together.
- Most importantly, the social origins of scientific knowledge are not relevant to its content, because that content is determined by nature or the physical world itself, not by cultural or social factors.

As we have suggested, it is as a result of these beliefs that sociology came to be concerned not with the actual content of science, but only with its social conditions, only with answering questions like 'How did it arise?' and 'Whose interests does it serve?' One of the results of this limitation was that much of the early sociology of science was a sociology of error rather than of truth. What these sociologists of knowledge seem to be saying to us is, 'Hey, there's no point having a sociology of what we already know to be legitimate knowledge. We bump into good old legitimate knowledge every day as we work and of course we leave it be. What we need is a sociology which explains why people believed, and still believe, non-scientific things, you know, stupid things.'

In the light of this, it is no surprise that Robert K. Merton, the person who really got the sociology of science going, studied the normative aspects of science and scientists' practices, rather than the content of science. Merton (1970) is famous for describing the 'ethos of science' in Weberian terms: the growth of Puritanism quite accidentally furthered the growth of science, mainly because the values of Puritanism and science coincided – utility, rationality, empiricism, individualism and asceticism; Puritans who were 'intellectuals' (probably an anachronistic term) tended to concentrate on issues of this world, and commit themselves to rational, methodical and impersonal investigation; out of this Puritan morality emerged a scientific ethos. In Merton's words:

> The mores of science possess a methodological rationale but they are binding, not only because they are procedurally efficient, but because they are believed right and good. They are moral as well as technical prescriptions. Four sets of

institutional imperatives – universalism, communalism, disinterestedness, organized skepticism – are taken to comprise the ethos of modern science. (1973: 270)

Once again, it would be hard to underestimate the power of this viewpoint in defining what sociologists of scientific work took to be their 'home ground'. In virtually all other fields of knowledge, apart from science, sociologists of knowledge were happy to problematise knowledge on the basis of how it was produced: thus, liberalism, for example, or Kantianism, or Keynesianism, were readily impugned because they were not seen to be scientific (in Marxist terms, these bodies of knowledge belong to the realm of ideology).

A great epistemological mountain range had to be crossed before scientific knowledge – as opposed to science – could be subjected to thorough scrutiny. The crossing of this mountain range allowed the development of the Foucaultian-inspired study of science at the heart of this and the following chapter. Our background picture is not complete until we recount this crossing. The main explorers in this part of our story were not sociologists – as we've just seen, they were too timid – but philosophers.

The important explorations of some philosophy of science

Up until about 1960, philosophers of science, like their sociological counterparts of that era, believed that scientific knowledge was the crowning glory of human reason. Karl Popper was at the forefront of this thinking; Popper and his contemporaries (for example, Carnap), believed, *inter alia*, that:

- there is a distinction between observation and theory;
- knowledge is cumulative – science is evolving, producing more correct theories;
- science has a tight deductive structure;
- scientific terminology is or ought to be precise;
- science is a potentially unified enterprise – all the sciences should have the same methods.

Popper's central question was 'What are the real sciences?' For example, is psychoanalysis a real science in the way physics is? Popper found his answer in a method he termed falsificationism – only real sciences put themselves on the line and risk being shown to be wrong. To be a science, a knowledge enterprise must allow all its claims to be tested by shared, widespread methods such that each and every claim might be shown to be false. If a claim is not open to falsification, the knowledge enterprise from which it comes is not a science (see, for example, Popper 1963).

In the early 1960s this line of thinking was seriously challenged by the work of Thomas Kuhn. In a now famous book called *The Structure of Scientific Revolutions* (1970) Kuhn disputes pretty much all that Popper held dear, arguing that the distinction between observation and theory in science is not as clear as Popper suggested, that science is not cumulative, that sciences do not have tight deductive structures, that scientific concepts are no more precise than non-scientific ones, that science does not have a methodological unity – indeed, different sciences are not unified in methods – and that sciences are historically specific rather than universal.

Kuhn claims science is cyclical, the cycle taking the following form: normal science–crisis–revolution–new normal science–crisis–revolution– new normal science– and so on. 'Normal science' is about 'puzzle-solving' (pretty much exactly what it says) within an established group of theories or 'paradigm', as he labels related groups of theories. Within each paradigm new theories are constructed. Each paradigm is slowed by anomalies – problems with the theories. Scientists working within the paradigm try to make small amendments to the theories to have them overcome the anomalies. In other words, science, for Kuhn, is the process of attempting to explain certain objects to which it is directed by paradigms in terms of the theories of whichever paradigm is dominant at the time. It is not the dispassionate business of verification and falsification that Popper claims it is.

In the Kuhnian account of science, differences between paradigms are enormous, like the differences between religions. Scientists working within one paradigm do not even have access to a common language with which they might talk to scientists working in another paradigm (this is what Kuhn calls the incommensurability of paradigms). From this perspective scientific knowledge is not cumulative knowledge; there is no sense of science building an ever more complete picture of reality for the benefit of humankind. Rather, any piece of scientific knowledge has to be considered as the product of a certain place and time – it makes sense at the time and in the place, but at a different time and/or in a different place it may make no sense, it may even be completely forgotten. Even what gets measured is subject to this sort of dynamic shift. For example, nineteenth-century chemists worked out precise atomic weights (for example, calculating that the atomic weight of chlorine is 35.453) but in the 1920s different scientists, using a different paradigm, worked out that naturally occurring elements are a mixture of isotopes. Chlorine (on earth) comes in isotopes with atomic weights of 35 or 37 and it is the ratio of these isotopes that gives chlorine its specific weight on earth. Once you understand this, then finding out the precise weight of chlorine on earth becomes less important. No one bothers measuring atomic weights any more (Hacking 1990).

'Do you think all this background is helping?' Iva asks Martina, a slightly plaintive tone to her voice.

'Sort of,' came Martina's half-hearted reply. 'I guess it'll be good for us in the long run.'

'You mean like that silly gym work you had us doing last year?'

After more giggles Iva got serious again. 'I suppose I want to hear Foucault's name mentioned occasionally, just to reassure myself I'm still in the right place. And when are we going to meet Monsieur Latour?'

Although Foucault and Kuhn were unaware of each other's work, the similarities between them are striking. While we have already stated that, for us, Foucault is crucial to the more recent development of the study of science at the heart of this chapter, we acknowledge that it was Kuhn who got the ball rolling for this approach by so forcefully calling scientific essentialism into question.

It is at the mention of the term 'scientific essentialism' that we worry that you may be squirming, maybe even committed Foucaultian students like Iva and Martina are squirming just a tiny bit.

'I'm not sure about this essentialism business. It sounds like a nasty disease', Martina said, only partly joking.

Iva displayed another burst of her steely determination (a very helpful quality for good students). 'Let's keep working through it for a little while longer tonight. This looks like it's going to help us track down the mysterious Latour.'

'Okay, at the very least it should help us see why all the other Foucaultian nuts who turn up to these meetings say 'science, science, science' in every bloody sentence.'

Scientific essentialism and the problem of representation

In dealing with 'scientific essentialism', Steve Woolgar (1988) suggests we focus on the following:

- the idea that science is something special and distinct from other forms of cultural and social activity, despite the impossibility of arriving at a definition of its distinctiveness;
- the popular view of science whereby objects of the natural world are taken as real and as enjoying an independent pre-existence to the extent that the social origins of scientific knowledge are considered irrelevant to its content;
- the notion of 'great men' who discover these 'real-world' objects.

Scientific essentialism is a problem for Foucaultians inasmuch as it is (we hope you see this one coming) another way of hiding the content of science from the scrutiny of close study. You will be helped in overcoming this problem if you come to grips with the Foucaultian approach to the notion of representation.

The crucial thing to remember here is that everything we know we know through representation. It is impossible to demonstrate the existence of a fact without the intermediary of representation. Think for a moment about a phenomenon like electricity. We never directly access electricity (not even if we get plugged into the mains); we know of its existence through its effects or representations.

Scientific essentialism would have us believe that by direct observation we can side-step representations. But this proposition misses the role of representations in the practice of observation. Even observation is not direct access to the phenomena of the natural world, because even observation involves representation. For example, one current theory of vision holds that photons move from an object and strike our retinas. We then have to do all kinds of work (the brain has to turn the image received by the retina the right way up, etc.) to change this information into a *representation* (in they come, through the back door).

In other words, 'seeing' does not give us direct access to truth and fact. We can now sensibly answer questions like, 'Why did Galileo not see with his telescope the things Copernicus saw with his?' Galileo's telescope theoretically allowed him to see just as much (or as little) as Copernicus saw through his. A sensible answer must focus on representations, that is, on the different ways Galileo and Copernicus worked on objects in order to turn them into different representations. A Kuhnian would answer that the different paradigms within which Galileo and Copernicus worked had a determining effect on what representations might arise. We hope you can see that a Foucaultian attempt to deal with this problem, although it would use a different vocabulary, would not reach a wildly different conclusion. To think about this a little more, have a look at the early pages of *The Order of Things*, where Foucault (1970) describes how wildly different the world looks to the inhabitants of different epistemes (an episteme is something like a way of understanding the world which is specific to a time and place – a set of understandings which enable sense to be made of the world).

Let's get back to representations. Woolgar (1988) argues that when scientists are confronted with the inevitability of the problem of representation (that is, the problem that their knowledge is not unmediated and therefore may be accused of being corrupted), they try to wriggle out of their difficult position in a variety of ways:

- They can appeal to a hierarchy of knowledge (for example, physicists claim that a voltmeter accurately reflects voltage in ways that a dream cannot indicate meaning for a psychoanalyst). For Woolgar (and for us), this perception of relative reliability can be understood as a *consequence* of natural science's claimed superiority in establishing correspondences, not its *cause*; that is, physicists here are merely *asserting* the superiority of their measuring instruments (and, hence, their proximity to the essences of the world) based on a belief in their own discipline's superiority. The problem of the relation between the representation and the essence is no less real.

- They can pretend the problem is a local difficulty (for example, we just need to build better instruments to capture the truth of the world).
- They can pretend the problem doesn't exist, or if it does, it is someone else's problem.

For us, the best way to deal with the inevitability of representations is to build an awareness of their role into a new account of the process of scientific discovery. In doing this we must first be clear about what is involved in 'discovery'. Let's consider a famous 'discovery': Christopher Columbus and the discovery of America (for more details, see Brannigan 1981).

Columbus spent twenty years organising his mission to the presumed east coast of the Indies. He struggled to raise funds and was regularly turned down by Portuguese and Spanish Crowns, the latter only relenting after he managed to scare them into thinking they would lose a military advantage if they did not fund his mission.

Columbus and his team made very specific assumptions about what they were going to discover: they knew where the land mass was going to be; they knew they would meet natives (they stocked up on trinkets, beads, buttons, etc.); and they budgeted for a round trip of 4,000 miles in terms of food supplies. In other words, the character of the soon-to-be-discovered-object had already begun to be shaped. Representations were at work.

Once they had discovered the lands, Columbus and his crew then had to manoeuvre for institutional backing for the discovery. On the return journey, they dropped bottles into the oceans with messages about the discovery. At this stage, Columbus's claim was that he had discovered some islands off the east coast of the Indies. On reaching home, Columbus put a lot of effort into publications communicating the news and eventually the Vatican agreed to Spanish claims for the lands.

Even from this small example it is clear that 'discovery' is a process, rather than an instant in time. It involves planning, anticipation, gaining support and obtaining institutional approval. To put it another way, for the budding Columbuses among you, you haven't discovered anything unless you get 'the authorities' (obviously different authorities in different cases) to agree with you. When we say that Columbus discovered America, we are opting for a particular version of a story sanctioned by specific authorities.

Furthermore, the process extends in time both before and after the initial claim of discovery. Columbus made further voyages to the 'islands' he thought he had discovered. Ten years later Amerigo Vespucci claimed to have discovered an extended land mass, countering Columbus's discovery of 'islands'. Vespucci's claim was initially resisted because of certain Christian notions about the earth being uniform and known.

Eventually Vespucci's version held sway, but Columbus's achievement was rewritten by the historians of the sixteenth century. This was in spite of the fact that other 'discoverers' also had claims to have found the new continent: Siberians, Phoenicians, the Irish, the Norse, and many others. None of these discoverers had Columbus's resources or the abilities to organise the 'discovery' story.

Subsequently, the Columbus story has become legitimated through entrenchment: Columbia University, Columbia Pictures, and so on, are all strong reminders that Columbus was *the* discoverer of America. It is almost impossible to overthrow the version of history which says Columbus discovered America – one would have to overcome popular beliefs and prestigious histories.

Also, it is not merely a case of arguing about who discovered a specific object. We are not arguing that someone else (for example, Vespucci) 'really' discovered America; the point is that the character of the discovered object is the *result* of this long process of definition. Vespucci and Columbus did not discover the same object – in a sense, they discovered radically different things. We should not presume that an object pre-exists our efforts to get access to it. Rather, the definitional work that discoverers do shapes the discovered object itself.

Iva and Martina are starting to feel more at ease with the Foucaultian excursion into science, though they're hardly without worries.

'Hey, Martina, is this what you remember about science from high school?'

'You've got to be kidding. I barely remember attending a science class. I had better things to think about . . .'

'Yeah, I know what you mean. But through the fog I can still hear Mr Smithers droning on about observations and experiments.'

'Hey, you're right; we're swimming along nicely but we haven't dealt with all that 'very scientific' stuff yet.'

We can sort out these worries for Iva and Martina, about some of the techniques of science, though it's not always easy-going.

A Foucaultian account of observation and experiment

Typically, scientists carry out observation, experiment and the analysis of the data in the laboratory and its environs. The 'nature' or 'reality' which scientists deal with in the laboratory is 'highly preconstructed, if not wholly artificial' (Knorr-Cetina, 1981: 3). Experimental rats are supplied from specific 'clean' sources, blood is obtained from the specialised companies which serve science, and so on. It is important to note that the laboratory and all the substances in it are the product of human effort.

For an experiment to formally 'discover' a new scientific truth, it must be replicable, that is, other scientists must be able to conduct the same experiment and achieve the same results. However, the replication must be neither exactly the same, nor too different. If it is exactly the same, it is said to be really the same experiment, not adding to our knowledge (that is, if it is identical in every respect, even in terms of when it was conducted and by whom, then it literally is the same experiment). The most minor difference would be the same experiment conducted again a short time after the first by the same team (that is, another in a 'run' of experiments). This experiment would have less confirmatory power than an experiment which had more differences. For example, if a result obtained on one set of apparatus was found again by a different team on a completely different set of apparatus, this would be good news for the scientists involved, because they could be confident that the apparatus had not caused the result (that is, the result is not an artefact of the apparatus). But this process cannot go too far.

If the differences between experiments in a replication are maximised, we can have some extreme possibilities. A finding in theoretical physics backed up by a gypsy examining a goat's entrails (Collins 1985) would not have a powerful confirmatory effect, for example. A powerful replication, then, lies somewhere between least and most differences from the original experiment.

But, just when you thought it was safe to go back into the argument, things are even more complex than this when we go to another extreme. A more powerful replication is one that involves *disconfirmation* – this is one that is most like the original (in the extreme case, the original experimenter looks again at the reading and revises his/her own 'first impression'). In other words, the more different an experiment is, the easier it is to claim that the differences caused the second experimenter not to obtain the results of the first. What is regarded as appropriate changes to an experiment must be socially negotiated. Clearly the gypsy/goat entrails scenario is unacceptable, but only because it has been decided in advance what is acceptable/scientific experimental practice.

We can say that, in lay terms, the notions of replication, experiment, neutral statistics, observation, and so on, are science's attempts to lay its cards on the table. However, we must also add that there are certain tacit knowledges and unexplored (unacknowledged) practices that allow science to continue. In the selection of confounding variables (differences between the experiments which are suspected of causing different results), certain variables will not be considered confounding. For example, if you mix together potassium and water one day and do a replication the next, it's unlikely that you'll consider the fact that you were wearing a different wrist-watch confounding. Of course, if your experiment involved you using your watch to time the chemical interaction, the wrist-watch might become a variable. The problem is, as we hope you can see, that what counts as a variable depends on what scientists decide is important enough to count. It can be argued that these selections work in favour of the status quo of science.

We can see this point more clearly if we simply consider attempts by 'normal' science to discredit 'paranormal' science (Collins and Pinch 1979). A frequent tactic used by 'normal science' in this battle is to argue that paranormal findings cannot be given credence because it is theoretically possible to achieve those findings fraudulently (note that it is not suggested that a fraud is actually committed in these circumstances). So, for example, the way in which the Uri Gellers of this world (as well as more serious scientists of the paranormal) can be belittled is by showing what sleight of hand could have been used to achieve the 'paranormal' results. Collins and Pinch's counter-argument is that, of course, if this criterion were applied universally, no scientific knowledge could ever be generated, because it would always be possible to imagine our scientists are fraudulent, doing the scientific equivalent of marking the deck of cards. Again, a perspective not unlike the Kuhnian looks attractive here: paranormal scientists, because they are outside the 'club' (the paradigm), are evaluated according to different (and frankly non-scientific) criteria.

Let's look at a specific example of the social negotiation of the good experiment, taken from Collins (1985): Joseph Weber's claims for the existence of gravity waves. We'll try to keep the 'science' to a minimum. Gravitational radiation can be thought of as the invisible equivalent of light or other radiation. Most scientists agree, following conventional astrophysics knowledge and Einstein's general theory, that massive moving bodies will produce gravity waves, but only waves so weak that their detection is very difficult. However, it is generally agreed that violent events (exploding supernovae, black holes, etc.) in the universe lead to gravitational radiation, or fluxes of gravity waves which are theoretically detectable on earth because they affect g – the constant that is related to the gravitational pull of one object on another.

Gravitational pull attracts objects to each other. The earth's pull is enough to keep us stuck on it; our own gravitational attraction to each other (person-to-person gravitational pull) is something similar but is too weak to make us stick together (lucky for us). Scientists can just about measure gravitational attraction, but measuring gravity wave fluxes is incredibly difficult because the fluxes lead to tiny fluctuations within the force of attraction.

Weber designed an apparatus to measure this effect. A huge aluminium bar is measured for changes in gravitational attraction between its (internal) parts – the apparatus tries to measure tiny movements within its subatomic structure as a pulse of gravitational radiation passes through. Because the radiation is an oscillation, the bar 'rings' if its dimensions are exactly right. Weber set up a device which allowed this oscillation a connection to the production of a voltage. This tiny voltage can be amplified and recorded on a pen chart. Insulation techniques are used to negate the effects of electrical, magnetic, thermal, acoustic and seismic forces. However, because the atoms of the bar are continually vibrating randomly, one always gets some reading on the pen chart (this is random thermal 'noise' – atoms vibrate if the ambient temperature is above absolute zero).

One then has the problem of deciding what readings to count as instances of gravity waves. In general, a high peak is an indicator, but one has to decide how high the peak must be to be counted. However high the level is set, one gets false negatives and false positives. Weber claimed to be finding several peaks (about seven) every day. His claims were sceptically received – because he found far too many. If there was as much gravitational radiation around as he was claiming, there would be so much energy in the universe that it would quickly burn up. Weber's findings looked alright, but nobody accepted them because theory and observation are so closely linked. It is not possible to accept the findings without rewriting astrophysics, which nobody was or is able or prepared to do.

As Collins notes, at this point one has the problem of the 'Experimenter's Regress':

1 Are we getting correct results from our experiment?
2 This depends on whether gravity waves are hitting the earth in detectable fluxes.
3 To find this out we need to build a good gravity wave detector.
4 We'll know if we've built a good gravity wave detector if we get correct results.
5 But are we getting correct results?
6 We go back to (2) and continue circling around for ever.

Collins suggests that the only way to break this circle is to find some other means of judging the experiment: a criterion independent of the outcome of the experiment. As Collins shows, this 'independent' judgement of scientific work, as the way out of the regress, is daunting. It is almost impossible to come up with scientific criteria which allow one to comment on the value of an experiment. As such, scientists often use different criteria to judge the quality of others' scientific work, especially the following:

* faith in the honesty and capability of other scientists;
* the personality and intelligence of other scientists;
* the 'laboratory reputation' of other scientists; the background, in industry or academia, of other scientists;
* the previous history of success/failure of other scientists;
* gossip about other scientists;
* the size and/or prestige of the university from which the research emanates; and so on.

In the case of Weber's work, scientists just did not believe in the existence of such high fluxes of gravity waves. Various reasons were given as to why Weber was wrong (problems with his computer programming, for example). A growing literature of negative results was collected, but as well a group of experimenters set out to deliberately 'kill' Weber's findings in a bid to have only negative results count as serious contributions to the debate. This concerted effort to dismiss Weber's findings was one of the ways a particular scientific controversy was able to reach a closure (Weber's research is flawed).

Once again, what can be seen in this example is that the movement from representation to object is not a straightforward one and is only accomplished as the result of a lot of work by human actors. What counts as a good experiment is socially negotiated. Observation and experiment rely on tacit knowledge, such that they are never purely neutral. In certain cases special rules of experimentation may even be required.

'Things are looking clearer', Martina chirruped, feeling happy with herself.

'Clear as a glass of that famous Latour red,' Iva replied in a mocking return chirrup. They both broke up. 'We must be getting tired if we find that so hilarious,' Iva added. 'Maybe if we have a rest and come back to it tomorrow, we'll be in better form to catch the mysterious wine-maker turned Foucaultian superstar.' They turned in amidst more laughter.

Latour in a black box

In *Science in Action*, Latour (1987) explicitly portrays scientists as entrepreneurs, indiscriminately chasing political, scientific and economic goals. He suggests that one of the ways scientists make their way in these various fields is by 'black boxing'. The notion of the black box is a useful one for us to bear in mind in disputing the self-evidence of scientific objects. 'Black box' is a term used in cybernetics: when something is too complex to be fully explained or represented, a black box is drawn to replace the complex arrangement; arrows indicate what goes into the black box, and what goes out, but the actual contents and workings of the box are not examined.

Latour argues that when something has been 'black-boxed', it is simply used in a chain of arguments. For example, the DNA helix is a black box: scientists have calculated how it works, but it has been closed up and is, at least to a certain extent, immutable. Other scientists now assume the inviolability of the DNA helix and treat it as a black box: they do not open it up, but they do describe relations to it, drawing arrows in and out. We can easily expand this notion of black boxing to other areas of life, outside of science. For example, when we drive a car, we are engaging in a certain amount of black boxing. The precise workings of the engine are probably not known by us – someone else has done that work – and our input to this technological system is probably limited to the level of filling the tank with petrol and knowing which pedals to push, as well as making a few minor running adjustments. Perhaps we can describe our driving in a simple diagram:

(Basic driving/car maintenance knowledge) → [automobile technology] → (Ability to move from A to B)

In this 'socio-technical system' (a mixture of the social and the technological), we are only concerned with our input (learning to drive, steering the wheel, changing gear, etc.) and the output (quick, convenient travel). The black box is what we rely on in the middle and what we do not examine.

Now that you've worked your way through all that background and, at last, been introduced to Latour's Foucaultian method of dealing with some aspects of science, it's time for you to tackle another exercise.

EXERCISE 3.1

Please draw two other diagrams of 'black-boxed' aspects of everyday life. You might like to choose from: using medical services, using a computer, using the telephone. But of course you should feel free to select your own examples. When you've finished the diagrams, please write a short essay (500 words), using what we've told you so far, giving more details about how the aspects of everyday life you've selected are 'black-boxed'.

Now we can return to Latour's description of what scientists get up to when they do their work. Latour suggests that the biggest and most successful scientific constructions are put together by assembling more and more black boxes. In our example above of the automobile technology, we could break down the central black box into a series of smaller ones which are piled up on top of each other (the internal combustion engine, side-impact bars, airbags, the gearbox, etc.). Some black boxes may be 'leaky'; that is, they are not left completely unexamined, but may be tampered with and improved. However, as long as actors act as if the black boxes are sealed, the construction can continue.

Black boxing is a way of simplifying the social world. Even if we limit ourselves to the world of automobiles, we can quickly see just how complex it is, involving technologies (cars, traffic management systems, radar traps), rule systems (the highway code) and humans. Black-boxing elements of this system make it possible for innovators and users to get on with their jobs.

Working in conjunction with Michel Callon, Latour uses his work on science to make a more general methodological point relevant to other investigations. This point concerns the actors involved in social life. Whereas much social science research wants to draw a big distinction between macro-actors and micro-actors (at its most extreme this distinction is that between society as macro and individuals as micro, but it expresses itself in other less extreme forms as well), for Callon and Latour, macro- and micro-actors are roughly the same in kind. The main difference is that a macro-actor is sitting on top of a lot of black boxes. To speak of macro-actors is to engage in a necessary process of simplification (that is, to do black-boxing work). Macro-actors can only work effectively if they involve many simplifications. Indeed, Callon and Latour suggest that another important difference between macro- and micro-actors for their purposes is that macro-actors are much simpler (see Callon and Latour 1981). At this point we would note that to a certain extent both Callon/Latour and Foucault urge a kind of simplification of social analysis: Callon and Latour want us to stop the old habit of thinking that the micro and the macro are different in kind, while Foucault attempts to show us how the same organisational unit – the statement – is the building block for all kinds of ventures (big, little, successful, failed).

An example derived from Callon (1986a), which continues our motoring theme, should help clarify these ideas. *Electricité de France* (EDF) were struggling to launch an electric vehicle in the 1970s. Their goal was to bring the ideal electric vehicle into existence. In lobbying for the usefulness of this innovation, EDF black-boxed the evolution of industrial societies. They worked from the assumption that unless the all-out consumption ethic of the postwar years was checked, the human race's happiness and quality of life was doomed. The consequence of this black boxing was that for EDF, the internal combustion engine, with all its attendant pollution risks, needed to be replaced by the electric vehicle.

Having black-boxed the future of transport in general terms, EDF now laid out a future chronology, assigning roles to particular manufacturers: the early vehicles were to be powered using lead accumulators until 1982; from 1982 to 1990, zinc–nickel accumulators were to be used, along with the zinc air circulation generator; from 1990, fuel cells were to be used. EDF attempted to black-box a number of beliefs and future scenarios with which manufacturers, interest groups, governments and the general public were invited to identify. They constructed these scenarios from a variety of sources: nature (catalysis, components of fuel cells), the economy (costs of cars, the market for buses, etc.) and culture (urban life, *homo automobilis*, fear of pollution).

The future seemed to be decided; but another actor was to break open some of the black boxes. Renault, the car manufacturer, was given a fairly minor role in all of this by EDF – as the manufacturer of chassis for the new vehicles. Renault, in this scenario, were in trouble, because they were to be turned from a major manufacturer into a bit player. During the first few years of the project they were unable to fight back, because so many people had been convinced that the electric car was the future. If Renault wanted to fight back, they needed to open up some black boxes. And this is indeed what they did.

EDF had argued that no one would want a thermal car any more. Yet even while oil prices went up, the demand for cars increased. Renault began to suggest that the desire for a thermal car would carry on regardless of increasing oil prices and *alongside* a desire to reduce pollution and congestion. Renault then began to translate the consumers' demands differently, suggesting they wanted the speed, comfort and acceleration an electric car could never deliver. In this way, Renault opened the black box, albeit only slightly, of social evolution that EDF had constructed. Renault suddenly realised they had won this battle; very few people actually wanted to drive a glorified milk-float, no matter how much EDF tried to convince them of its environmental and economic benefits. With this success, Renault started opening other black boxes. The idea that the internal combustion engine was a dead end was opened up and Renault even went so far as to suggest instead that the use of advanced electronics could perfect the internal combustion engine so that it could become unbeatable for several decades to come.

In this story of the battle between Renault and EDF, a series of black boxes were constructed and then broken apart. Yet often in science, there are just too many black boxes to be opened – too much effort is required to take the work apart. We note in passing that Callon's analysis of this event did not assume in advance that science and technology are separable; his approach enables us simply to follow the development and resolution of a techno-science controversy.

To return to our earlier example of gravity waves, the apparatus that Weber built picked up not just gravity waves but also thermal noise from the aluminium bar. The dissenter was able to say that Weber may well have been picking up gravity waves, but he was picking up something else as well – and that 'as well' was enough to destroy his work. Weber was unable to black-box his equipment, to make it an unquestioned, unexamined part of the procedure of unequivocally measuring gravity waves.

To work from a different example, taken from Latour (1988), in the early days of microbe science, microbes were grown in urine. It was very hard to see the microbes and arguments followed as to whether they were really present. Later, a solid milieu culture was invented, such that microbes showed up in colour against a white background. This removed the possibility of any argument about their presence (that is, a black box was formed). Latour suggests that the best laboratories are the ones with the most black boxes, where the least dissent is possible. And the macro-actors are simply the actors who have a lot of black boxes underneath them.

In Latour's account, science is understood as a kind of war, with all the protagonists attempting to get more and more allies on their side, that is, to enrol other actors. Enrolment is necessary, because if you do not enrol other actors, your work will be limited to yourself, to a single point in space. EDF attempted to enrol Renault, to give them a specific job which helped out in the construction of a specific scenario, that of the electric vehicle. Latour suggests that enrolment works by the translation of interests; put crudely, you have to convince people to want what you want. In practice, this proves very difficult and actors have to engage in a variety of tactics to make it happen. We discuss two tactics here (there are more in Latour 1987).

Tactic 1: Displacing goals. Sometimes it is necessary to invent a problem so that your solution becomes appealing. In the early 1940s Leo Szilard talked to the Pentagon about building an atomic weapon, but they were not interested. They argued that it would take too long to develop a new weapon system. Physicists would be better off spending their time perfecting the current weapons systems. What Szilard did was to change their goals. He asked the Pentagon what they would do if the Germans got the atom bomb first; how could they win the war with their obsolete weapons? The politicians still had to win the war, but it was no longer just the war they were intending to win (a conventional weapons war) – it was the war envisaged by the physicists, who now became necessary to the war effort. So, Szilard was able to translate the Pentagon's interests by displacing their goals (see also Szilard 1978).

Tactic 2: Inventing new goals. Szilard's move was a nice one, but there was a limit to what he could persuade the Pentagon to do; as Latour puts it, he wouldn't have been able to persuade them to lose the war or support classical dance; his scope was limited by the original aim of winning the war. In some situations this would not be enough. For example, George Eastman moved into the business of selling photographic plates, but he soon realised he had a very limited market. His plates and his paper were only of interest to a few professionals and well-equipped amateurs. Others were uninterested in taking photographs. What Eastman had to do was invent a new market, and he did this by inventing the idea of amateur photography. Everyone from six to ninety-six could and should want to take photographs. To enrol people into this scheme, Eastman had to make the process simple and cheap, something which he succeeded in doing. As the slogans have it: 'You press the button and we do the rest'; or in France, 'Clic, clac, merci Kodak' (see Jenkins 1975; Latour 1987).

In summary, the reception, acceptance and development of science and technology depends to a great extent on a series of practices in which the scientist is a multi-faceted entrepreneur, indiscriminately mixing economic, political, natural and cultural claims to construct truth. In Latour's (Foucaultian) vision of this process, the construction of knowledge is the result of epistemological strategies like black boxing. However, it is never enough, in his view, to construct scientific knowledge; it is also necessary to enrol other actors to your point of view. The main method for doing this is the translation of interests. A stable scientific situation is one with plenty of black boxes and a relatively unproblematised set of shared interests. Once the translation of interests breaks down, then the black boxes are attacked by dissenters (like Renault, or Weber's opponents). A strong piece of knowledge will be black-boxed further and further back.

'I'm not too sure about the terminology,' Iva put in playfully.

'I suppose we can always translate it into more academic-sounding language,'

Martina continued her banter, 'though it's a shame to spoil such interesting material with such dull language.' The expected giggles followed.
  'It's almost our duty,' Iva concluded with a wicked grin.

Resisting determinism

One of the things that is attractive about the work of Latour and his colleagues in this new 'science studies' approach, for our way of thinking in any case, is that it avoids giving any kind of theoretical or methodological primacy to things, words, technologies, ideas or humans. It is particularly gratifying that they avoid the idea of determination by technology, a sort of worshipping at the feet of scientific technology that so often afflicts the study of science. Having said this, we still have to discuss some of the problems with determinism.

It is easy to regard technologies as having a particular 'impact' on society which society cannot resist, or to regard technology as the inevitable result of a set of (political, economic or other) interests. The perspective we are outlining here is that technological systems are the embodiment of complex social, cultural and political assumptions. In this argument, technology and society mutually condition each other. Rather than think of technology as an independent given which affects or is affected by social development, we can think of it as part of a continuously developing dynamic system.

In fact, if we start to think about a definition of the word 'technology', this mutual relationship becomes clear. An object can only be technological if it forms part of a set of human activities. A computer with no programs or programmers is merely a collection of metal and plastic; it is only technological when it becomes immersed in the world of human activity. As Mackenzie and Wajcman define it (1985: Introduction), a technology must be a simultaneous mixture of physical objects, human activities and knowledge (the latter because technological things are useless without the know-how to use and repair them).

Technological determinism is a very common way of thinking about the impact of technology on society. For example, Lynn White (1962) has argued that the invention of the stirrup determined the development of feudal societies. The stirrup enabled warriors on horseback to be a much more effective fighting system, melding the man and the horse into a single unit. White argues that this new way of doing combat was not only very effective, it was also very expensive; it required extensive training of men and horses, and the production of armour. To support this elite fighting force, society was completely reorganised into a feudal form.

At first glance, this is a compelling account, but there are problems with seeing the stirrup as determining the advent of feudalism. First of all, a technology may be available, but it does not have to be taken up. The characteristics of a society play a major role in deciding which technologies are taken up. Second, the same technological object may be taken up with different effects in different societies. The stirrup 'caused' feudalism among the Franks, but it did not have this effect among the Anglo-Saxons prior to the Norman Conquest.

In similar vein, we can think about the eighteenth-century revolution in weaponry in France and eventually the rest of Europe. New techniques for making cannons were envisaged and eventually put into place. These made cannons more efficient, lighter and more accurate. In essence, this changed the nature of warfare because it put more stress on a rational artilleryman who could make all the various calculations required to kill an enemy half a mile away. This did not sit easily with older notions of prowess and heroism which were, until then, dominant understandings of what made up a soldier. Eventually that notion died out (with some resistance) as modern warfare became less and less about individual prowess and courage. What we can see in this example is the way in which social desires and technological invention constantly condition each other.

The opposite view, which is also frequently espoused, and which you have probably realised makes the same error, is to assume that technology is shaped by science. This way of thinking entails a causal model: science → technology → society. But science and technology do not have such a one-sided relationship. Many technologies were invented in circumstances that owed little or nothing to existing science (for example, the spinning jenny, the plough, the watermill, the steam engine). Furthermore, it can be argued that the impact of technology on science has been as great as that of science on technology. For example, without the computer, many modern sciences could scarcely function. We should redraw the above model of science, technology and society as a circle of mutually conditioning entities. Technologies, then, are resources which can be used, and in being used, they lead to a reorganisation of the whole 'sociotechnical system'. Technological systems are always being constructed and reconstructed.

To consider a more homespun example, in the field of education, there is a dynamic relationship between technologies that are made available and the types of teaching that are done. Teaching needs 'demand' a whole series of new technologies to increase the impact of teaching (overhead projectors, 'smart' lecture theatres, 'powerpoint' presentations, use of video and on-line resources, etc.). These technologies were to some extent demanded by teachers, but they also forced teachers to revise their teaching methods (for instance, teachers now readily photocopy materials instead of dictating to students). In addition, the new technologies give rise to other new technologies (the use of overhead transparencies allowed for the development of computerised overhead transparency production software programs).

There are plenty of technologies which seem to offer great possibilities, but which are never taken up. The self-cleaning house, the centralised vacuum cleaning system, the Betamax video system and the gas refrigerator are all prominent examples. Let's consider the gas fridge in more detail, drawing on the account of Cowan (1985). In principle, in the early decades of the twentieth century, the gas fridge seemed like a perfect solution to the problem of refrigeration, especially in the domestic market, where gas was cheaper than electricity for many homes. Other advantages of the gas fridge included: it lacked moving parts, which meant that it required virtually no repair or maintenance; it would last virtually for ever; and it was silent (the electric fridge was, at first, incredibly noisy – in fact, fridge manufacturers have still not completely eliminated the noise problem; early electric fridges were so noisy they would often be kept in the basement, well away from the living quarters).

So how did this inferior product, the electric fridge, defeat the gas fridge? One important factor was that General Electric, the company that marketed the first domestic fridges, wanted the electric fridge to succeed for economic reasons. It was in their interest to develop the all-electric kitchen. General Electric (along with the electric utility companies) engaged in an aggressive marketing campaign, including financing a film (*Three Women*) with big Hollywood stars of the time (Sheila Mannors, Hedda Hopper, Bert Roach and Johnny Mack Brown). This film, made in 1935, was, improbably, a comedy/romance based around the complete electric kitchen. But making a film was only one strategy: General Electric set up a whole series of other publicity stunts. In one such stunt, displays of pirates' treasure chests were organised in prominent department stores and it was mysteriously announced that they would be opened on a particular day. Keys were distributed to selected neighbourhoods. Amid much pomp, the boxes were opened (by the local mayor and other dignitaries) to reveal the latest General Electric fridge. Puppet plays were put on – inside fridges. In 1928 a fridge was taken to the North Pole by submarine with Robert Ripley (originator of B*elieve It Or Not*). By these strategies, General Electric translated the interests of consumers, other manufacturers and electricity utility companies, and in doing so the less aggressive and poorer gas fridge companies were eliminated.

In this example, the various available technologies were developed in accordance with other non-technological factors around them – the gas fridge could not take off because it was not marketed aggressively and because the companies that promoted it, like Servel, lacked the financial resources of General Electric. In addition, the myth of the electric kitchen as the modern, clean kitchen was very powerful. However, the technology was also constantly reshaped and refashioned to fit with new demands (for example, it was made more compact to move from the basement to the kitchen; it was made quieter, etc.).

Another important point here is that while it is misleading to study technology independently of these other elements, we also need to study the way in which the social contexts are simultaneously reconstructed by the chosen technology. In particular, Callon (1986a, 1986b) suggests that the translations that take place in socio-technical systems invent what he terms a geography of obligatory points of passage. For example, anyone wanting to develop fridge technologies now has to pass through the electric fridge

– the gas fridge has become closed off. Thus the social landscape is altered unless someone can find a way of circumventing the point of passage, which can only be done by reopening the black box, as with our earlier example of the electric vehicle; it was an obligatory point of passage which Renault managed to open up again.

Let's see how you get on applying these ideas to your own example.

EXERCISE 3.2

Using our account of the gas fridge as a model, please write your own brief account (500–1,000 words) of the decline of some other piece of 'failed' good-quality technology. Two other examples are the eight-track cartridge music system and Betamax videos, but please feel free to use other examples, if you know enough details. Your main aim in this piece should be to show the mutual conditioning of the social, the economic, the scientific and the technological. You might also like to show how something becomes an obligatory point of passage (for example, video developments now have to go through VHS; Betamax is closed off to the point where new video cassette developments have to be 'backwards-compatible' with old-fashioned VHS cassettes). Please try to frame your account so it is 'problem-based'.

Summary

'Okay, we're there at last. We now know something about Latour. Are we ready to go back in and face the music?' asked Iva in a summarising mood.

'Depends what music,' replied Martina, unable by now to talk about any of this science business without a feeling of levity. 'A quiet Foucault waltz I could face, but Foucault disco – no way.'

Iva's determination to summarise was broken by a good chuckle, but it soon returned. 'I'll tell you what – let's make a list of everything we've learned about following scientists around with a Foucaultian shovel and then decide whether we're ready for the next of those dreadful reading group meetings.'

They drew up the following lists:

- Foucault's methods have been used to deal with an increasing variety of intellectual objects in recent years.
- One of the more noteworthy of these is science; Foucaultian methods are heavily involved in a new approach to science studies.
- Foucault's concern with knowledge is very different to standard socio-logical concerns. Sociology of knowledge has traditionally made a special case of science and exempted its production of truth from

investigation. Inspired by Foucault's methods, a group of thinkers, featuring Latour and Callon, has turned this approach on its head, focusing on the ways science produces truth rather than exempting it from scrutiny, and focusing on the *constructedness* of science.

Quite a lot of background is necessary to appreciate the scope of and emphases of this new science studies approach:

- The form or content of scientific knowledge was once considered off-limits to sociology, which traditionally regarded scientific knowledge as objectively true and therefore not interesting to investigate.
- This trend continued well into the twentieth century, especially with the development of a specialist branch of the discipline – the sociology of knowledge.
- This standard approach to the sociology of science can be summarised, albeit crudely, in four propositions:

  (a) The natural world is real and objective. Observers do not effect its qualities.
  (b) Although the natural world is undergoing a certain amount of change, there are underlying universal, permanent aspects.
  (c) Because science has evolved stringent techniques for the observation of phenomena and the formation of laws of the universe, we can be confident about the empirical evidence gathered by scientists to help us put those laws of science together.
  (d) Most importantly, the social origins of scientific knowledge are not relevant to its content, because that content is determined by nature or the physical world itself, not by cultural or social factors.

- In this way, we can see that the *social context* of science is at the heart of this sociology of science, not its *content*.
- A big change was needed to break out of this way of thinking, and the big change came through philosophy, not sociology.
- The big change occurred in the 1960s. Before this, philosophical thinking about science concentrated on a series of basic propositions: there is a distinction between observation and theory; knowledge is cumulative – science is evolving and eradicating error; scientific terminology is or ought to be precise; science is a potentially unified enterprise – all the sciences should have the same methods.
- Kuhn's *Structure of Scientific Revolutions* is an important marker of this 'big change'. This book and the thinking it generated suggested a very different set of basic propositions: there is no sharp distinction between observation and theory; science is not cumulative; sciences do not have tight deductive structures; scientific concepts are not particularly precise; science does not have a methodological unity, indeed, different sciences are not unified in methods; sciences are historically specific. Kuhn developed a characterisation of science as cyclical –

normal science interrupted by 'revolutions' leading to new normal science, and so on.

- Kuhn and Foucault worked at the same time but were unaware of each other's work. Nonetheless, there is a striking similarity between their opposition to scientific essentialism: the idea that science is something special and distinct from other forms of cultural and social activity; the popular view of science whereby objects of the natural world are taken as real and as enjoying an independent pre-existence to the extent that the social origins of scientific knowledge are considered irrelevant to its content; the notion of 'great men' who discover these 'real-world' objects.
- Involved in the opposition to scientific essentialism is a Foucaultian rethinking of the notion of representation, particularly the role of representations in the practice of observation.
- Scientists try to side-step the inevitability of representations by appealing to a hierarchy of knowledge and/or pretending the problem is a local difficulty and/or pretending the problem is someone else's problem.
- Rather than side-stepping this inevitability, for the Foucaultian approach, it is better to build it in to a new understanding of the process of scientific discovery.
- Turning to aspects of everyday scientific conduct like observation and experiment, it can be argued that they involve a certain artificiality, particularly in regard to replicability.
- In all this, we can see that science attempts to 'lay its cards on the table', but we can also see that it keeps behind its back some tacit knowledges and some unacknowledged practices. These are especially clear if we examine attempts to discredit paranormal science (a more detailed example is the treatment of Joseph Weber in regard to his claims to have discovered gravity waves).

Our discussion of Weber led to an enunciation of the problem of 'experimenter's regress', and the ways scientists typically try to overcome this problem.

- Latour's notion of 'black boxing' makes more sense against this background. This involves leaving elements out of consideration (for example, in driving a car we know about only some elements of the car – the black box is what we rely on but do not examine).
- Black boxing helps scientists go about their work, especially in simplifying the complexities of the social world.
- In collaboration with Callon, Latour uses these insights to break down the distinction between macro- and micro-actors. The various Latourian points introduced thus far are illustrated by the example of a development of the electric car in France, whereby EDF (*Electricité de France*) failed to introduce the electric vehicle.

- Whereas in this example most of EDF's black boxes were eventually opened, especially by Renault, in most scientific examples there are simply too many black boxes for them to be opened. Weber's gravity waves 'discovery' serves as a good example again here, as does the 'discovery' of microbes.
- In keeping the lids on so many black boxes, science employs two main tactics – displacing goals and inventing new goals.
- A big advantage of the Latourian use of Foucault's methods is that it avoids technological determinism. Accounts of the changes wrought by the development of the stirrup or of certain weapons are instances of this type of determinism.
- The Latourian approach shows how science, technology and society are mutually conditioning. The development of the gas fridge provides a good example.
- From this example we can see an important point of Callon's very clearly – the translations that take place in socio-technical systems invent a geography of obligatory points of passage. New developments must work through those which have come to dominate (for example, the development of any new fridge technologies must now work through the electric fridge).

'Heavens above', exclaimed Martina when they were done compiling these lists, 'we really have covered some ground'.

Iva had to agree. 'Yes, we're ready for the next instalment of the reading group alright . . . But . . .'

'Oh no, not another one of your famous pregnant pauses,' Martina complained with mock seriousness.

'You know what I mean,' Iva went on, 'we're better prepared, but not satisfied. I've grown to quite like a glass of this Latour, but we've hardly had more than a sip. I know we needed all that background, but now that we've arrived at Latour Land I want to do more exploring.'

We'll leave Iva and Martina to sort this one out for themselves. We hope you feel the same way as Iva. You've done the hard work in getting to know some of the basics about the Latourian use of Foucault's methods. In the next chapter we take you through some more Latourian possibilities.

4

'Have I missed something? Modernism seems to have come and gone and yet never appeared, and power and knowledge seem to have become door-closers and crustaceans'

CONTENTS

'What on earth does he mean by telling us we've never been modern?'

Devon was exasperated almost to the point of anger. He's that type of student. He did an extremely good first degree and is now finishing off a PhD. He puts his heart and soul into his studies, to the point where it infuriates him if he can't understand something he really wants to understand.

His friend Dermot is a different type of character altogether. Laconic in manner and far from hard-working, he's been 'completing' his PhD for ages with the finish-line nowhere in sight. His interest in intellectual matters comes and goes with the breeze. When it comes, he appears to everyone who hears him talk or who reads his notes (he never seems to write anything more than notes) to be remarkably gifted, capable of understanding the nuances of the most complex debates

with seemingly little effort – possibly the reason his university tolerates his hap-
hazard ways. He barely looked up from the TV at Devon's outburst. Perhaps he
enjoys frustrating Devon, but you can never tell.

Dermot hadn't really said much to provoke Devon, just thrown him a copy of
Latour's We Have Never Been Modern *and said it was good. This was enough.*
Devon had heard all about Latour and was determined to 'sort him out'. He'd read
a couple of Latour's earlier essays and thought they were pretty good, but, as
always with Devon, the essays were just enough to whet his appetite. Another
friend had told him Latour had recently summarised many of his arguments in
We Have Never Been Modern, *so he'd bought a copy. He didn't get far into it*
when his frustration took over. He'd recently decided, after poring over it for many
months, that Foucault's Archaeology of Knowledge *should be read as a cri-*
tique of modernism and was being grudgingly admired at the fortnightly post-
graduate seminar for the way he doggedly posed this reading of Foucault. He had
a firm position on modernism and here was Latour undermining it. He'd left the
book with Dermot yesterday afternoon in disgust.

Dermot hardly ever bothered with the postgraduate seminar, so he didn't really
know about Devon's achievement in summarising modernism and its shortcom-
ings. He'd half-heard him prattling on about the matter several times while they
were having coffee together, but as he was reading the sports pages each time
Devon raised it, he'd barely listened to him. He wondered, inasmuch as he ever
wondered about such things, why Devon got so worked up about Latour's basic
meaning on simply being given back the book this morning and being told it was
good. Dermot simply had no idea how annoying his manner could be.

Devon tried to catch his frustration before it got the better of him. He turned
the conversation away from Latour's meaning and toward Dermot's reading,
hoping he could salvage some calm by establishing that in truth Dermot had been
too slack to even pick the book up. Big mistake.

'How much of it did you read?'

'All of it,' Dermot replied with his trademark tone, managing to turn and face
Dev for the first time since he'd come in, admittedly because of an ad break in the
football coverage.

Devon's inner demons got on their bikes and started to have a wild time in his
mind. He demanded to know what was in the book, and when Dermot began
calmly to tell him, he had to storm out. Dermot barely noticed as the ad break fin-
ished and the coverage resumed.

Devon was right to sense the importance of this book. It does capture
much of what Latour has done with Foucault's methods and is a very
useful source for us as we try to round out our picture of the Latourian
approach to scientific knowledge. Devon's frustration was unnecessary.
Despite some bizarre French touches – Latour admits (1993: ix) his book
is Gallic in a way that might be galling to some English-speaking readers
– the book is quite approachable. While we can't be quite so laid back as
Dermot, we can give you a reasonably relaxed summary of the book, in

the first section of this chapter, before returning to Latour and Callon's more detailed investigations of science at work. We hope our summary will help Devon as well as you, but we can only wait and see.

We Have Never Been Modern: a summary

Doubts about modernism, antimodernism, premodernism and postmodernism

Latour (1993) spends a good deal of energy defining and re-defining his principal target, modernism, or, to be more accurate, the markers used to stake claims to being modern – he makes the astute observation that the modernist account of modernism is just that – the modernists' own account; just as the history of the French Revolution can be understood as a product of that 'revolution', to the point that it was only ever a revolution in the 'revolutionaries'' terms, so modernism has only ever been modern in terms set up by the modernists (1993: 40). He tells us that the boundaries between the natural, the social and the discursive, which seem so real, are what mark the modern (1993: 7). Furthermore,

> 'modern' designates two sets of entirely different practices which must remain distinct if they are to remain effective, but have recently begun to be confused. The first set of practices, by 'translation', creates mixtures between entirely new types of beings, hybrids of nature and culture. The second, by 'purification', creates two entirely distinct ontological zones: that of human beings on the one hand; that of nonhumans on the other. (1993: 10–11)

Another definitional angle Latour explores concerns modernism's approach to temporality. 'Modern time is a series of inexplicable apparitions attributable to the distinction between the history of sciences . . . and just plain history' (1993: 70). On the basis of this point, he suggests that 'the moderns' have falsely constructed two different histories, producing a distinction between 'the contingent and the necessary'. This leads to the dominance of revolutionary thinking; this is the only way the moderns can conceptualise history – as revolutions. 'The asymmetry between nature and culture then becomes an asymmetry between past and future' (1993: 71). 'Progress and decadence are their two great resources, and the two have the same origin – their "systematic cohesion" which gives the impression that time passes' (1993: 72). And this passing, revolution-prone time is marked by crisis: modernists take a 'morose delight in being in perpetual crisis and in putting an end to history' (1993: 114).

Modernism is also sometimes defined by its confusions. For example, 'The moderns confused products with processes. They believed that the production of bureaucratic rationalization presupposed rational bureaucrats; that the production of rational science depended upon universalist scientists' (1993: 115–16). Another example concerns modernism's obsession with causes. This produces some absurd use of nouns as adjectives and adverbs. Words like '"science", "technology", "organization", "economy" . . . are good nouns, but they make lousy adjectives and terrible adverbs'. Scientists only use them in this way, he argues, because they have been put into their mouths by 'sociologists and epistemologists' (a theme we return to later) (1993: 116).

Another of these defining confusions of modernism is that it continually seeks to push the local to the global, not appreciating that the global can only ever be dealt with locally. 'There are continuous paths that lead from the local to the global, from the circumstantial to the universal, from the contingent to the necessary, only so long as the branch lines are paid for' (1993: 117). The modernist myth of the universal suggests that science 'always renews and totalizes and fills the gaping holes left by the networks in order to turn them into sleek, unified surfaces that are absolutely universal' (1993: 118). This last confusion has proved remarkably persistent. The moderns 'thought there really were such things as people, ideas, situations that were local and organizations, laws, rules that were global' and they thought this in regard to the social as well as the natural (1993: 120). He adds that attempts to address these totalities by totally revolutionising them have produced 'those modernists *par excellence*, the Marxists' (1993: 126).

Latour sets out what he calls the 'Constitution of the moderns'. This is made up of three guarantees, though he warns that the first two would make no sense without the third:

1 'even though we construct Nature, Nature is as if we did not construct it';
2 'even though we do not construct Society, Society is as if we did construct it';
3 'Nature and Society must remain absolutely distinct; the work of purification must remain absolutely distinct from the work of mediation' (1993: 32, fig 2.1).

Latour goes on to tell us that the moderns, crucially, have a fourth guarantee in their 'crossed-out God' – a God who is there without being there, who can be believed in without having Him intervene inconveniently in their thinking about Nature and Society. In providing the final link in a chain of checks and balances which makes modernism so powerful – the moderns 'have not made Nature; they make society; they make Nature; they have not made Society; they have not made either; God has made everything; God has made nothing; they have made everything' (1993: 34) – the moderns relied on the Reformation to give them such a convenient God, a God which one ultimately only had to know in one's heart, allowing them to be both secular and pious at the same time' (1993: 33).

Latour is very much aware of the awesome critical power of modernism. After noting that this power is currently fading (he knows that he could not have written his book were it not), and pointing out that modernism's power to be critical lies at the heart of many forms of indignant critique, Marxist and other, Latour summarises:

> Solidly grounded in the transcendental certainty of Nature's laws, the modern man or woman can criticize and unveil, denounce and express indignation at irrational beliefs and unjustified dominations. Solidly grounded in the certainty that humans make their own destiny, the modern man or woman can criticize and unveil, express indignation at and denounce irrational beliefs, the biases of ideologies, and the unjustified domination of the experts who claim to have staked out the limits of action and freedom. (1993: 36)

He is impressed with the moderns' speed of hand – they 'hold all the critical possibilities, but they displace them from case to case with such rapidity that they can never be caught redhanded . . . they are, they have been, they have almost been, they have believed they were, invincible' (1993: 39).

'I can't follow it, I can't follow it!' Devon shouted to himself and at himself. He had decided to dip back into We Have Never Been Modern *for the bizarre reason of trying to impress Dermot. He hadn't told Dermot he was reading the book again and had visions of impressing the socks off Dermot one day by bursting in on him and telling him he could follow it. Dream on.*

What can you do with a mind set like Devon's? Mmm, tough question. Just let him get on with his own little world, we suppose.

Latour's definitions of modernism all point in the same direction: modernism has collapsed, to the point where we should question whether it ever arrived (and, of course, answer, 'No, it did not'). He tells us the moderns are 'victims of their own success. . . . The modern Constitution has collapsed under its own weight, submerged by the mixtures that it tolerated as material for experimentation because it simultaneously dissimulated their impact on the fabric of society' (1993: 49). He goes on to tell us that the 'moderns have caved in. Their Constitution could absorb a few counter-examples, a few exceptions. . . . But it is helpless when the exceptions proliferate' (1993: 50). The temporality of the moderns has also collapsed – 'The proliferation of quasi-objects has exploded modern temporality along with its Constitution' (1993: 73) – and so too has the very ground of its philosophical defenders. These modern philosophers are more like 'pre-postmoderns [in that they] raise what had only been a distinction, then a separation, then a contradiction, then an insurmountable tension, to the level of incommensurability' (1993: 59).

The turn to antimodernism or premodernism or postmodernism is also futile. While he acknowledges that the collapse of the Berlin Wall in 1989 gave encouragement equally to those interested in modernism (both its domination and its emancipatory potential), those interested in antimodern or premodern reaction, and those interested in postmodern scepticism (1993: 8–10), Latour is equally dismissive of them all. He says of antimodernism that it 'struggles fiercely against the effects of the [modern] Constitution, but accepts it fully. . . . Only the sign and the direction of their indignation vary [from the moderns]. . . . The antimoderns, like the postmoderns, have accepted their adversaries' playing field' (1993: 47–8).

Latour fleshes this out later in his text: 'The antimoderns firmly believe that the West . . . has truly peopled the social with cold and rational monsters which saturate all of space' and 'saturate' other processes as well. Where modernists celebrate these 'saturations' as 'glorious, albeit painful, conquests', antimodernists see the situation as 'an unparalleled catastrophe'. However, but 'for the plus or minus sign, moderns and antimoderns share the same convictions' (1993: 123). In regard to antimodernist defences of 'the margins', he says these presuppose totalitarianism. He points out that this ignores the fact that any totals are built from locals. 'Look for the origins of modern myths, and you will almost always find them among those who claim to be countering modernism with the impenetrable barrier of the spirit, of emotion, the subject, or the margins' (1993: 124).

Of premodernism, Latour tends to use it to help situate modernism. 'By saturating the mixes of divine, human and natural elements with concepts, the premoderns limit the practical expansion of these mixes. It is the impossibility of changing the social order without modifying the natural order – and vice versa – that has obliged the premoderns to exercise the greatest prudence' (1993: 42). He argues that premodernism serves modernism well as an 'other': 'The internal partition between humans and nonhumans defines a second partition – an external one this time – through which the moderns have set themselves apart from the premoderns. For Them, Nature and Society, signs and things, are virtually co-extensive. For Us they should never be' (1993: 99–100).

Postmodernism is quite a target for Latour. He tells us that postmodernism refuses the task of empirical description as 'scientistic' (modernist), yet it accepts the modernist idea of dividing time into successive revolutions, leaving it in the 'ludicrous' position of coming after the moderns while arguing against the idea of any 'after' (1993: 46–7). Postmodernists, Latour proposes, 'really believe . . . that scientists are extraterrestrials, that matter is immaterial, that technology is ahuman, that politics is pure simulacrum. . . . [Postmodernists are] simply stuck in the impasse of all avant-gardes that have no more troops behind them' (1993: 62). Later in his book, Latour emphasises the theme that postmodernism is merely a symptom:

> [P]ostmodernism is a symptom, not a solution. The postmoderns retain the modern framework but disperse the elements that the modernizers grouped together in a well-ordered cluster. The postmoderns . . . are wrong to retain the

framework and to keep on believing in the requirement of continual novelty. (1993: 74)

Perhaps surprisingly, Latour thinks quite a bit of postmodernism can be salvaged from this wreckage for his nonmodernist approach. We return to this point shortly.

'I can follow it, I can follow it,' Devon enthused as he burst in on a particularly unenthusiastic Dermot. 'I've been working through it again and I'm now seeing connections with those debates in philosophy of science we used to talk about.'

Devon is right. Of course, many of Latour's arguments assume a detailed knowledge of the operation of science in society (for example, that modernists confuse products with processes to the point that they believe the production of rational science depends upon universalist scientists). They assume that his readers are familiar with a literature which has long debated the role of rational science in society and the possibility of universalist scientists. Latour can make this assumption because this literature – loosely grouped as the history and philosophy of science literature, briefly discussed in the previous chapter (see, for just the most obvious examples, Popper 1959, 1963; Kuhn 1970; Lakatos and Musgrave 1970; Feyerabend 1975) – is indeed remarkably familiar to a readership far wider than a specialist science in society readership.

Dermot was in no mood to be charitable.
'Change the channel before you go out please Dev. And let's talk about this when you've got past the bleeding obvious.'

Towards a nonmodernist methodology

Divisions   As we have already glimpsed, Latour is keen to break away from false divisions. He believes modernism is characterised by an 'odd' division – 'let us not mix up knowledge, interest, justice and power . . . [;] on the left they have put knowledge of things; on the right, power and human politics' (1993: 2–3) – and characterises his work and that of his 'friends' (the new science studies approach at the heart of these two chapters) as an attempt to break down this divide while studying science. He says these studies of science are not studies of the scientific objects themselves, being more about the ways they merge with the 'society' of which they are part; nor are they studies of merely contingent politics, being more about the combination of 'collectives and objects' (1993: 4–5). The other false divisions Latour seeks to overcome include that between the local and the global, that between nature, society and the discursive, and that between science and politics. We need not revisit his discussion of the local/global dualism. On the other two divisions listed he has quite a lot to say.

On the division between science and politics Latour takes us back to the famous seventeenth-century air–pump debate between Boyle and Hobbes. Drawing on the analysis of Shapin and Schaffer (1985), he argues that Boyle and Hobbes actually invented the division itself (Latour 1993: 16). While this debate looks like a non-debate at first glance – Boyle's political views match Hobbes's and Hobbes's commitment to mathematical methods for science match Boyle's – the two are a long way apart when we put science and politics together. Boyle's experiments with the air-pump eventually relied on the invention of the experimental method – the careful observations of a group of scientists – still used today. Hobbes's political theory, seeking to overcome the disastrous effects of civil war via the idea of commitment to the authority of a ruler without recourse to a higher authority (God or spiritualism), runs counter to Boyle inasmuch as Boyle's proof by scientific gentlemen suddenly provided a new escape route from the authority of the sovereign (1993: 16–20).

Latour provides his strongest hint about how to overcome the effects of the division between science and politics when he tells us that the significance of Shapin and Schaffer's work lies in part in their denial of the importance of context *per se* in favour of a focus on the messiness of the laboratory. They show, he says, how Boyle answered Hobbes not through a move to the macro level which Hobbes demanded, but by conducting more and more laboratory experiments, by attempting to prove Hobbes wrong by the evidence of the laboratory, thereby extending judgements on the evidence of witnesses to include the 'evidence of things', things to do with the laboratory and with experiments. This meant, Latour stresses, a dramatic shift away from the certainty of universals (1993: 20–4).

In elaborating this position, Latour argues that Shapin and Schaffer are too close to a Hobbesian position. They use terms like 'interest', 'power' and 'politics' quite innocently, not taking their deconstruction to the point they do with Boyle. Were they to do so, he says, they would see that it was Hobbes himself who invented the modern use of these terms (1993: 25–7). In this way, Latour wants us to see that, together, Boyle and Hobbes invented the modern world. 'Hobbes and Boyle quarrel in order to define the two resources that we continue to use unthinkingly' – that 'the representation of nonhumans belongs to science, but science is not allowed to appeal to politics; the representation of citizens belongs to politics, but politics is not allowed to have any relation to the nonhumans produced and mobilized by science and technology' (1993: 28). The descendants of Hobbes and Boyle are each involved in translation, but of different types – 'the political spokespersons . . . translate their principals, who cannot all speak at once', while 'the scientific spokespersons . . . translate their constituents, who are mute from birth' (1993: 29).

Sociology and anthropology Latour makes several methodological points about sociology which are potentially relevant to our purposes here. In seeking to overcome the effects of the division between nature and society,

Latour sees sociology as a hindrance rather than a help – it contributes to this division through its perpetuation of the idea of a separate sphere of the social. For Latour, sociology produces a dichotomy between objects and society whereby society is a double basis for denunciations – first by being so strong as to determine everything about objects, and then by being so weak as to be completely determined by objects, depending on the requirements of the particular site of denunciation. This is the basis, he says, for all society/other dualisms (like society/individual or society/community), in some hard/soft combination. These dualisms, he says, provide '99 per cent of the social sciences' critical repertoire' (1993: 53–4).

In overcoming this problem, Latour tells us that his and his colleagues' science studies approach has discovered that society is built of objects. This approach uses the critical repertoire of the social sciences against the hard side of each dualism, and this has brought the dualism down and wiped out the critical repertoire (1993: 54–5). Latour is convinced that sociology can dispense with distinctions between knowledge, belief and science (1993: 94) and can thereby dispense with the need to be critical. His aim is to emulate some work by Boltanski and Thévenot (see, for example, 1987) which, he says, provides an escape from the imperative to unmask (that is, always to be trying to reveal something supposedly hidden) and proposes a 'sociology of criticism' in place of 'critical sociology' (1993: 44). It is worth noting in passing that Boltanski and Thévenot here are very close to Garfinkel's insistence that the documentary method of interpretation ('unmasking') is a *lay* activity.

The appeal of these arguments is perhaps easier to see when we push on and consider some of Latour's insights about anthropology. It seems his approach is more akin to anthropology, but only when anthropology is in the field, that is, when it is gathering information about other cultures. He says anthropologists have no problem seeing things in networks when they are dealing with 'other' societies, but cannot do the same to their 'home', western societies. They cannot because the boundaries between the natural, the social and the discursive seem so real to them, trapped as they are within modernism (1993: 7). He commends Shapin and Schaffer's study of the Boyle/Hobbes debate for being the first to put history of ideas and the context of science together via 'the world of practices and networks' (1993: 20). Anthropology 'at home', or rather 'of home', Latour argues, makes a false distinction between humans and non-humans. He says it can be rescued by being made 'symmetrical', made to give up the asymmetry of sociology of knowledge and epistem-ology which together have promoted yet another false division, this time between true and false science, not allowing the techniques for examining true knowledge to apply to false knowledge (as we saw, in another context, in the previous chapter), forcing us for instance to account for false knowledge through such devices as ideology (1993: 92). Latour wants sociological studies to follow the lead of a certain type of ethnologist:

[E]very ethnologist is capable of including within a single monograph the definition of the forces in play; the distribution of powers among human beings,
gods, and nonhumans; the procedures for reaching agreements; the connections
between religion and power; ancestors; cosmology; property rights; plant and
animal taxonomies. The ethnologist will certainly not write three separate
books: one dealing with knowledge, another with power, yet another with practices. (1993: 14)

By Latour's new 'nonmodernist' method, comparative anthropology
'no longer compares cultures, setting aside its own, which through some
astonishing privilege possesses a unique access to Nature. *It compares
natures–cultures*' (1993: 96, emphasis in original). It thereby begins to treat
'home' in the way it treats the 'tropics'. The proposed 'symmetrical anthropology' 'uses the same terms to explain truths and errors . . . it studies the
production of humans and nonhumans simultaneously . . . finally it
refrains from making any *a priori* declarations as to what might distinguish
Westerners from Others' (1993: 103).

We hope that you are beginning to see some of the connections between
Foucault's and Latour's problem-based approaches – both suggest to us
that the analysis of a problem needs to cross certain boundaries. Now it's
your turn to think about a research problem and its boundaries.

EXERCISE 4.1

For this exercise, we would like you to consider a research problem
you are either currently working on or are about to start. The task of
this exercise is to draw up a plan (about 500 words) for the analysis
of that problem which makes use of Latour's proposed symmetrical
anthropology. Please concentrate on the following:

- the simultaneous analysis of humans and nonhumans;
- the treatment of truth and error in the same terms;
- the refusal to treat phenomena you *think* you know about (e.g.
  society) as special cases: society is simply a network of objects;
- the refusal to distinguish between knowledge, belief and science;
- the refusal to make judgements;
- the refusal to 'unmask' – concentrate instead on the careful
  description of details.

Some more important concepts We now move on to Latour's complex
formulations about hybridisation, a particular approach to networks, and
the idea of symmetry. He tells us that if we pay attention to the hybridisation going on around us, we raise the possibility that we have never been
modern (1993: 11). His account of networks forms part of his attempt to
overcome the false division between the local and the global – 'The two
extremes, local and global, are much less interesting than the intermediary

arrangements that we are calling networks' (1993: 122). Writing on the principle of symmetry, Latour quotes Michel Serres: 'The only pure myth is the idea that science is devoid of all myth.' Latour picks up this baton and says we have to account for, for example, Pasteur's failures in the same terms as his successes. He shows us how the study of science can give up the array of explanatory devices for failure – 'Society, beliefs, ideology, symbols, the unconscious, madness' – at the heart of its asymmetry; 'a slimming treatment for the explanations of errors offered by social scientists' (1993: 93).

Latour develops these nonmodernist formulations in a variety of ways. For example, he says that giving up critique-based indignation does not mean giving up morality. Rather, it means recognising the 'unofficial morality' which 'does not allow indignation, but ... is active and generous because it follows the countless meanderings of situations and networks' (1993: 45).

Nonmodernism is not about 'entering a new era': 'we are no longer obliged to cling to the avant-garde of the avant-garde; we no longer seek to be even cleverer, even more critical'. He summarises:

> This retrospective attitude, which deploys instead of unveiling, adds instead of subtracting, fraternizes instead of denouncing ... I characterize as nonmodern. ... A nonmodern is anyone who takes simultaneously into account the moderns' Constitution and the population of hybrids that Constitution rejects and allows to proliferate. (1993: 47)

He goes on to ask, how can we make the series of shifts the nonmodern suggests – the world of objects to that of quasi-objects; immanent/transcendent society to collectives of humans and nonhumans, etc.? How can we gain access to networks? 'We have to trace the modern dimension and the nonmodern dimension' (1993: 77), we have to realise that the nonmodern approach aims to restore the 'mediating role to all agents' (1993: 78).

Later in his text Latour offers more discussion on the direction of these possibilities of nonmodernism:

> [B]y traversing ... networks, we do not come to rest in anything particularly homogeneous. We remain, rather, within an intra-physics ... we do not fall into immanence alone, since networks are immersed in nothing. We do not need a mysterious ether for them to propagate themselves. ... What sort of world is it that obliges us to take into account, at the same time and in the same breath, the nature of things, technologies, sciences, fictional beings, religions large and small, politics, jurisdictions, economies and unconsciousnesses? Our own, of course. (1993: 128–9)

Nonmodernism might, Latour says, be able to 'capitalize on the best resources of the modern critique'. There are four areas in this repertoire: 'external reality of a nature of which we are not masters', 'the personified forces which structure society', 'signification and meaning', and finally 'Being'. 'These resources are incompatible only in the official version of the Constitution. In practice, we have trouble telling the four apart.' These resources are not incompatible 'when we move from essences to events', when we focus on networks. The nonmoderns can thus put the four repertoires of critique together 'in the same networks'. 'The moderns are quite right to want reality, language, society and being all at once. They are wrong only in believing that these sets are forever contradictory' (1993: 88–9).

In this way, nonmodernism even allows us to 'escape from the post-modern prostration itself caused by an overdose of the four critical repertoires'. Latour asks a series of 'have you not had enough?'-type questions about our attitude to the modern critical repertoires, including the following about sociology: 'Are you not a little tired of those sociologies constructed around the Social only . . . because sociologists cannot cope either with the content of objects or with the world of languages that nevertheless construct society?' (1993: 90).

Another crucial feature of these nonmodernist formulations concerns the treatment of what it means to be human:

> [T]he human, as we now understand, cannot be grasped and saved unless that other part of itself, the share of things, is restored to it. So long as humanism is constructed through contrast with the object that has been abandoned to epistemology, neither the human nor the nonhuman can be understood. . . . A historical succession of quasi-objects, quasi-subjects, it is impossible to define the human by an essence, as we have known for a long time. . . . The human is not a constitutional pole to be opposed to that of the nonhuman. The expressions 'humans' and 'nonhumans' are belated results that no longer suffice to designate the other dimension. . . . The human is in the delegation itself, in the pass, in the sending, in the continuous exchange of forms. (1993: 136–8)

Latour takes us away from the use of simple causation without diminishing the importance of explanations and evidence; indeed he strengthens the disciplines of explanation and evidence through his reformulations. Latour again quotes Serres in rejecting the idea of causation: 'We want to describe the emergence of the object, not only of tools or beautiful statues, but of things in general' (1993: 82). He says,

> Serres ballasts epistemology with an unknown new actor, silent things . . . 'The word "cause" designates the root or origin of the word "thing".' (1993: 83)

And he goes on to argue that, 'Without accusation we have no causes to plead and we cannot assign causes to phenomena' (1993: 84).

'Serres who?' said Devon, again to and at himself, back into his usual mood of exasperation. He worried again and again about all the background knowledge that he didn't have. He worried most that Dermot would have this background

knowledge. 'What if Dermot thinks We Have Never Been Modern *is merely a prelude to some more difficult readings by Latour and co?' He went into a cold sweat at the very suggestion. Talk about a dupe of self-suggestion. He pulled himself out of the mire-of-his-own-making with his usual fantasy about how Dermot will shower him with enthusiasm if he sticks with it and sorts out his confusions.*

Latour's nonmodernist approach involves the production of (non-critical) explanations 'from the centre towards the extremes' (1993: 78).

> We do not need to attach our explanations to the two pure forms . . . Object or Subject/Society, because these are . . . partial and purified results of the central practice that is our sole concern. The explanations we seek will indeed obtain Nature and Society, but only as a final outcome, not as a beginning. (1993: 79)

Latour returns to the example of the air pump to help make his point that nonmodernism will not seek explanations at either of the poles of Nature or Society. Rather, it will explore this issue via questions like:

> How are the Royal Society's witnesses going to account for the leaks in the air pump? How is the King of England going to consent to let people go back to talking about the properties of matter and reestablishing private cliques just when the question of absolute power is finally about to be resolved? . . . [T]hese questions are no longer caught between Nature and Society, since they . . . redefine what Nature may be and what Society is. (1993: 80–1)

We have already seen the way Latour reformulates the notion of evidence through the use of this example. For Latour, evidence is not a naturally occurring adjunct to, or spur to, social scientific endeavour. Rather, techniques of evidencing need to be objects of inquiry in their own right. Nonmodernism will no longer allow us to assume that we know what evidence means for any particular inquiry; we must adopt the discipline of describing evidentiary procedures for each inquiry, whether we are conducting the inquiries ourselves or drawing on previously conducted inquiries. It is also worth pointing out here that there is a well-established tradition in the social sciences of conceiving techniques of evidencing as necessarily local (see especially Lynch [1993] and Silverman [1997] for various discussions which bear on this point).

In addressing the problem of relativism, Latour discusses two variations:

> Absolute relativism presupposes cultures that are separate and incommensurable and cannot be ordered in any hierarchy. . . . As for cultural relativism, which is more subtle, Nature comes into play, but in order to exist it does not presuppose any scientific work, any society, any construction, any mobilization, any network. It is Nature revisited and corrected by epistemology. (1993: 104)

Latour criticises anthropology for traditionally allowing 'modest relativism' while at the same time allowing 'the surreptitious return of arrogant universalism – we Westerners want to see ourselves as a special culture. . . . We Westerners cannot be one culture among others, since we also mobilize Nature,' we think we actually control Nature through science. 'Thus at the heart of the question of relativism we find the question of science' (1993: 97). He argues that the 'relativists have never been convincing on the equality of cultures, since they limit their consideration precisely to cultures'. The solution, according to Latour, 'appears along with the dissolution of cultures. All natures–cultures are similar in that they simultaneously construct humans, divinities and nonhumans' (1993: 106). Differences between cultures might be sizeable,

> but they are only of size. They are important . . . but they are not disproportionate. . . . The fact that one of the collectives needs ancestors and fixed stars while another one, more eccentric, needs genes and quasars, is explained by the dimensions of the collective to be held together. A much larger number of objects requires a much larger number of subjects. . . . If you want Hobbes and his descendants, you have to take Boyle and his as well. (1993: 108)

Absolute relativism, Latour goes on, has 'accepted the universalists' viewpoint while refusing to rally round it: if no common, unique and transcendental measuring instrument exists, then all languages are untranslatable . . . all rites equally respectable, all paradigms incommensurable' (1993: 112). He argues that this is not taking relativism seriously; it ignores the fact that the process of inventing measuring instruments is also the process of seriously inventing commensurability. What is needed, he says, is a 'relativist relativism' (what he later calls 'relationalism' [1993: 114]): 'The relativist relativists, more modest but more empirical, point out what instruments and what chains serve to create asymmetries and inequalities, hierarchies and differences. . . . Nothing is, by itself, either reducible or irreducible to anything else' (1993: 113).

Latour's nonmodern approach also provides a potential means of overcoming the confusions about temporality which, as we saw earlier, he regards as a defining feature of modernism. 'Time is not a general framework but a provisional result of the connection among entities' (1993: 74). As an example of this point, Latour says he uses both a drill and a hammer, yet one is thirty-five years old, the other hundreds and thousands of years. We all 'mix up gestures from different times' (1993: 75). 'We have always actively sorted out elements belonging to different times. . . . *It is the sorting that makes the times, not the times that make the sorting*' (1993: 76, emphasis in original).

What to salvage? At the end of his book Latour sets himself the task of summarising the elements of modernism, premodernism, postmodernism and antimodernism that are worth making part of his nonmodern approach. These summaries are rich and worth quoting in detail.

Of the moderns, he says, we might want to retain

> [t]heir daring, their research, their innovativeness, their tinkering, their youth-
> ful excesses, the ever-increasing scale of their action, the creation of stable objects
> independent of society, the freedom of a society liberated from objects – all these
> features we want to keep. On the other hand, we cannot retain the illusion . . .
> that moderns have about themselves and want to generalize to everyone:
> atheist, materialist, spiritualist, theist, rational, effective, objective, universal,
> critical, radically different from other communities, cut off from a past that is
> maintained in a state of artificial survival due only to historicism . . . denounc-
> ers always at war with themselves, prisoners of an absolute dichotomy between
> things and signs, facts and values. (1993: 133)

Of the premoderns:

> Let us keep what is best about them, above all: the premoderns' ability to dif-
> ferentiate durably between the networks and the pure poles of Nature and
> Society, their obsessive interest in thinking about the production of hybrids of
> Nature and Society, of things and signs. . . . On the other hand, we shall not
> retain the set of limits they impose on the scaling of collectives, localization by
> territory, the scapegoating process, ethnocentricism, and finally the lasting non-
> differentiation of natures and societies. (1993: 133)

Of the postmoderns:

> It is of course impossible to conserve their irony, their despair, their discour-
> agement, their nihilism, their self-criticism since all those fine qualities depend
> on a conception of modernism that modernism itself has never really practised
> . . . however . . . many of the intuitions of postmodernism are vindicated. . . . We
> can retain the deconstructionists' refusal of naturalization. . . . We can keep the
> postmoderns' pronounced taste for reflexivity but only if we strip them of their
> modernist clothing. Take away from the postmoderns their illusions about the
> moderns, and their vices become virtues – nonmodern virtues! (1993: 134)

Last, and very much least, the antimoderns:

> Regrettably in the antimoderns, I see nothing worth saving. Always on the
> defensive, they consistently believed what the moderns said about themselves
> and proceeded to affix the opposite sign to each declaration. (1993: 134)

Now for the moment of truth. Can you generate a list of nonmodern principles?

EXERCISE 4.2

Below is a list of things about modernism, premodernism, antimodernism and postmodernism Latour thinks should be changed. Please
go through the above summary of his *We Have Never Been Modern*
and identify Latour's alternative 'nonmodern' proposal for each of the

items on the list. Please summarise each one of his proposals in a sentence or two.

- Modernism draws false boundaries between the natural, the social and the discursive and another between science and politics.
- Modernism draws a distinction between humans and nonhumans.
- Modernism has a misleading approach to temporality.
- Related to this, modernism makes a false distinction between the contingent and the necessary.
- On a similar theme, modernism can only conceptualise history as revolutions.
- Modernism takes a 'morose delight in being in perpetual crisis and in putting an end to history'.
- Modernism confuses products with processes.
- Modernism is obsessed with causes.
- Modernism continually seeks to push the local to the global.
- Premodernism cannot see the possibility of changing the social order without modifying the natural order – and vice versa.
- Premodernism serves modernism well as an 'other'.
- Antimodernism and postmodernism have accepted their adversary's (modernism's) playing field.
- Antimodernism firmly believes that 'the West ... has truly peopled the social with cold and rational monsters which saturate all of space' and 'saturate' other processes as well.
- Antimodernism's defences of 'the margins' presuppose totalitarianism.
- Postmodernism refuses the task of empirical description as 'scientistic' (modernist), yet it accepts the modernist idea of dividing time into successive revolutions, leaving it in the 'ludicrous' position of coming after the moderns while arguing against the idea of any 'after'.
- Postmodernism is 'simply stuck in the impasse of all avant-gardes that have no more troops behind them'.
- Postmodernism is a symptom, not a solution.

'Okay, I'm done with that book,' Devon announced proudly as he burst in on Dermot once more. Unsurprisingly Dermot was camped in front of the TV.

Dermot wasn't in the mood to spare Devon his wit. Mind you, he's hardly ever in the mood to spare anyone.

'Perhaps now you're ready for the hard stuff,' he said quietly, without looking up.

Devon fought hard against his urge to take offence. He knew Dermot was winding him up. It was a tough battle for someone like Devon. Just about anyone can wind him up and Dermot of course can do it without even noticing.

Gathering his meagre resources in the sense of humour department, Devon replied.

'Oh yeah!'

Dermot appeared to ignore him. Completely emptied of humour in a flash, Devon could only ask Dermot what he meant by 'harder stuff'.

'Try some of the stuff about door-closers and seatbelts to start with,' Dermot said, without changing his tone from the clever-but-bored attitude that is his calling card.

Devon left quickly, determined to read more Latour if only to try to get ahead of Dermot. It's a vain hope, but as he might learn something along the way, it's worth our following him.

The problem of reflexivity

If you believe scientific knowledge is socially constructed, you may think you are in a position to use this belief to demonstrate the truth or falsity of scientific knowledge. If so, you need to check yourself at this point. To make this claim you've either not realised, or conveniently forgotten, that the social scientific knowledge on which you base your belief is itself subject to processes of social construction and negotiation. For example, in showing that the existence or otherwise of gravity waves is a matter of professional negotiation, our knowledge about this controversy is also subject to the same sort of negotiation. We can have no firm footing from which to make judgements about our accounts. We have to be wary of thinking that while knowledge about nature is subject to all kinds of prob-lematisations, social scientific inquiry is privileged (effectively a reversal of the 'standard' scientific view which assumes that social knowledge is flawed but knowledge about the material world is unproblematic). If we are to respect Latour's principle of symmetry we should treat both types of knowledge with equal circumspection (taking this or any similar step to address the problem is often said to involve reflexivity; put most simply, 'reflexivity' means applying a critical perspective to one's own knowledge claims).

We've already been introduced to the idea that for a Latourian/Fou-caultian approach we must be careful not to let reflexivity become rela-tivism. To make this point stick, we need to say a little more about relativism and its attractions. Especially since Kuhn's interventions, dis-cussed in the previous chapter, relativism has been a standard move when faced with the problem outlined above. In short, the basic idea of rela-tivism is that as we have no criteria for judging many competing know-ledge claims, we should make a virtue of not trying.

While this is a version of the ancient insistence on scepticism, it is not at all the same as the Pyrrhonian position we advocated in Chapter 1, as an important part of using Foucault's methods. This type of relativism is related to the Academic scepticism to which Pyrrhonism is strongly opposed. Where Pyrrhonian scepticism is based on the idea that we cannot know anything, *including the fact that we cannot know anything*, this type of relativism is based on the false certainty that we cannot know anything. This way of being a relativist leads to a kind of eternal circle of self-defeat.

The Pyrrhonian form of relativism, captured earlier in this chapter by Latour's delightful term 'relativist relativism', is well developed elsewhere by Callon and Latour (1992). They argue that extreme relativism eventually comes out as a form of realism; that is, if you start to grant things (nature) the same status you grant to humans (society), then you must eventually consider 'nature' an equal actor in scientific controversy. In doing this you are in danger of returning to scientists the sense of special authority the new science studies has done its best to undermine. As well, you risk granting objects the same status that scientists have traditionally granted them. Callon and Latour suggest that to be a social realist while at the same time refusing the claims of real objects involved in scientific disputes is to adhere to the same division between nature and society that sustains traditional scientific authority.

This is a good point to introduce you to Callon's fascinating discussion of scallops and fishermen, a discussion to which we return in greater detail in the next section. Basically, Callon argues that these two seemingly distinct groups – scallops and fishermen – should both be analysed as actors in exactly the same way, strongly advising against giving primacy to either one of these two or to any other actor in the network. For at least two of his critics, Collins and Yearley, this is asking too much: 'No ... study would rely on the complicity of the scallops; at best it could rely on human-centred accounts of the complicity of the scallops' (1992: 315).

Needless to say, we think these critics are missing something important here. To think that scallops have nothing to do with the story of science is empirically stifling, as we will see in more detail in the next section. If sociologists of science were just social realists, they would end up missing quite a lot. The corollary is also true: scientists can never simply be naive realists, as Collins and Yearley suggest they should be. If they were, they would never produce any facts – they would just be waiting around for 'truth' to bump into them. As we saw in the discussion of Columbus in the previous chapter, scientific discovery is an active process.

We have now had strong hints from both Latour and Callon that we need to develop an account of networks which treat humans and nonhumans equally. Unless we do this, we will not be able to recognise the closure of debates and the eventual non-negotiation of facts. Take, for example, Collins's (1985) account of the gravity wave controversy. He gives an unsatisfactory (from the point of view of the Latourians) account of how this controversy came to an end because he does not acknowledge the role of nonhuman actors (like gravity waves) in it.

If we are to treat Latour's and Callon's Foucaultian methodological interventions seriously, we need to understand that nonhumans are part of all disputes studied. We must avoid both downplaying and exaggerating their roles, but we do have to understand them as actants: open or closed, far away or near, wild or domesticated, depending on the result of their interactions in the network, in just the same way that we understand the role of humans.

'I've just heard Cathy prattling on in the seminar about scallops and fishermen. What the hell is she on about?'

Devon had been to the seminar, Dermot had not. So why would Devon seek out Dermot for advice. Who knows? The moth and the flame? The lemming and the cliff? Whatever, Dermot's flat is always where Devon goes when he feels intellectually puzzled (as we're quickly learning). And, of course, he always leaves Dermot's company feeling worse than when he joined it. This time was no exception.

'Don't you ever knock?' Dermot asked, more out of amusement than annoyance.

Devon was too perplexed about the scallops to treat the question seriously. He was prime fodder for a wind-up, but when is he ever not? Dermot couldn't resist.

'Latour and his mate Callon used to be scallop fishermen, diving in the Seine each weekday to scrape the little beggars off the bottom.'

'Are you serious?' Devon responded, realising as he said it that he'd walked into it yet again.

Dermot let him off lightly this time.

'For God's sake, Dev, get your head out of that We Have Never Been Bollocks *book and have a look at some of their other stuff.'*

Devon left straight away (as we're learning he so often does). Dermot knew he'd come back, in no more than a few days, after he'd read the recommended pieces, but still perplexed.

We can get in ahead of Devon again and work through some of this 'other' material in more detail. Again, we can avoid Devon's worries. It's not that difficult if you follow it carefully. We'll return to Callon on scallops and fishermen for more details and later go on to Latour on door-closers.

Scallops, fishermen and scientists – some details

Let's go back to the beginning of this fishy story – Callon's (1986b) paper on scallops and fishermen in a small French fishing area. Callon opens by reminding us that it is quite common for sociologists of science to treat nature as uncertain but society as certain. Society, for this way of thinking, always has the last word in determining nature, and without social norms, classes, and so on, science comes to a halt. This worries Callon and he suggests that to counter this sort of asymmetry we adopt a principle of symmetry in our analyses; as we saw above, this means assuming that society is as uncertain as nature. To do this most effectively we need to adopt another principle beside the symmetry principle, what Callon calls 'free association'. That is, we must abandon all a priori distinctions between natural and social events. In fact, Callon suggests (elsewhere) that divisions between nature and society, between nonhumans and humans, are the results of networks rather than their starting points.

Callon puts these principles into operation in his story of scallops and fishermen. Scallops are shellfish which are harvested in three places in France, including St Brieuc Bay. The amount of scallops was steadily dwindling in the 1970s because of a variety of factors, especially overfishing, climatic changes and predators (starfish). Callon begins both with this problem and, somewhat dramatically, with the end point ten years later, when a scientific knowledge of scallops had been introduced. Callon seeks to retrace the complex production of a network of relationships in which social and natural entities mutually controlled who they were and what they wanted, a network which included the aforementioned scientific knowledge.

Callon's paper follows three researchers who took part in the construction of natural and social facts in the case. They returned from a visit to Japan where they saw a similar species of scallop cultivated in 'collectors' to which the scallops anchor themselves and grow in an environment sheltered from predators. The obvious research question here was: 'Do the scallops in France anchor themselves in the same way as the Japanese scallops?' If they do, then the Japanese scheme was transferable to France.

The researchers began to construct a series of working definitions of the various protagonists: the fishermen, who would fish the scallops to extinction without scientific intervention; the scientific colleagues, who were interested in advancing knowledge about scallops; the scallops, who so far had only been seen as adults, but who were supposed to be able to anchor themselves when young to a collector; and themselves, who were 'basic' researchers. An important point here is that the initial problematisation touched on both the social and the natural worlds.

The researchers went on to define the ways in which all the actors had an interest in the proposed research programme. If the scallops wanted to survive, if the colleagues wanted to advance knowledge, if the fishermen wished to preserve their long-term economic interests, they had to know the answer to the question 'How do scallops anchor?', and had to recognise that their alliance around this question benefited them all. The question, then, became an obligatory point of passage, an idea we met in the previous chapter.

Up to this point the researchers had built up a model of a network, but this network had yet to be tested. The researchers attempted to make the network (of knowledge and actors) as strong as possible by the process of *interessement*. *Interessement* is the act of attempting to stabilise the identity of another actant by stabilising one's own links with that entity and weakening the links the entity has with other entities.

Scallops in the collectors were protected from predators, currents and other entities which threatened them. In addition, the devices used for *interessement* (in this case, the collectors) extended and materialised the hypothesis made about the scallops: defenceless larvae are threatened by predators; larvae can anchor; the Japanese experience can be translated to France because the scallops are basically the same. If this *interessement* were to be successful (that is, if the scallops were to flourish), then the validity of the researchers' problematisation had to be assumed. The researchers also 'interested' the fishermen (by meeting representatives) and their colleagues (by presenting material at conferences – graphs, diagrams, etc.). The *interessement* devices helped to construct a set of alliances and to shape and consolidate networks composed of both social and natural entities, humans and nonhumans.

But *interessement* does not always work; actants do not always accept the roles that are constructed for them. When they do, we can say that they have been enrolled, in much the way we saw in some examples in the previous chapter. If the scallops really did anchor onto the collectors, if the fishermen really did want to restock the bay and would desist from raiding the collectors, then we could say they were enrolled. In fact, the enrolments were not accepted. The scallops refused to anchor and some fishermen could not resist fishing the stocks the researchers built up. With these mutinies the character of the network, of the knowledge and of the actants, began to be transformed. The scallops' abilities to anchor were now cast into doubt; the fishermen's desire to see the long-term restocking of the Bay was likewise now a dubious proposition. In this case, social and natural phenomena were reorganised in the same way.

Callon suggests we can use this same framework to understand the closure of a scientific controversy: closure will occur if spokespeople are not questioned. In the above example the scallops did not obey their spokespeople – the first (few) larvae who did consent to anchor were not followed by their 'treacherous' fellow-scallops. The fishermen did not obey their elected representatives but put their short-term profit ahead of the long-term solution. Callon's doubts about scallops and his doubts about fishermen are of the same kind – nature and society, nonhumans and humans are analysed identically and symmetrically. Callon does not rely on a 'sociological' explanation (that is, one like Collins's [1985] description of the gravity waves controversy which privileges social factors in the ending of a controversy) of what is true; rather he prefers to follow a social and natural network through to see how what is true is put together.

The door problem

We now move on to a discussion of Latour's (1992) paper 'Where Are the Missing Masses?' The title refers to the so called missing mass in (some versions of) physics, whereby there is not enough mass in the universe to fit our theories of it. For Latour, there are missing masses in sociology too, and in the social sciences more generally, and they are nonhuman actants. There are lots of examples in his paper (seatbelts, keys, child car-seats, traffic lights, etc.), but we concentrate here on his discussion of the groom, or automatic door-closer.

Latour starts off by discussing the large amount of work delegated to the humble door hinge. The hinge helps us to enter and leave buildings and rooms with little effort and with little disruption to the comfortable climate of buildings and rooms – a lot of work for a nonhuman character. But there is still a problem here: how to keep the door closed when it's not in use. If it's not closed when not in use, you may as well have a hole in the wall, with its attendant disadvantages. One option is to discipline all building and room users so that they always close doors behind them. This is only a partial solution as it only takes one miscreant to undo the good work of the door and its hinge. Another option is to discipline just one person – a doorkeeper – whose express job it is to keep the door closed. This is a better option, but of course s/he may fall asleep, fall ill, go missing, such that the door remains open. The next move is to delegate the work to another nonhuman character, a sort of sibling of the hinge – a groom, an automatic door-closer which uses a hydraulic spring to shut the door.

The situation is not quite resolved yet, however. The groom is like a rude and badly educated doorkeeper: it will slam the door in your face unless you can acquire the skills to use it. An unskilled groom requires a skilled human user. Latour makes the point here that such nonhuman artefacts incorporate a morality; that is, they attempt to prescribe courses of action for weak and immoral humans (do this, don't do that, close this, drive slowly, etc.). He guesses in advance that we might object to the anthropomorphism of this account. He doesn't deny it, but rather goes on the offensive: the automatic groom is already anthropomorphic through and through. It is made by humans, it substitutes for humans, it gives shape to human actions. Feelings and desires are, literally, *incorporated* into the nonhuman delegate. In this case, it is merely the injunction to keep the door closed, but it can get more complex: electronic eyes can open doors as you approach, doors can ask you to prove your identity (with an electronic pass), doors can shut in dangerous situations (if equipped with smoke detectors, etc.).

For Latour, as we've discussed at several points, the distinction between human and nonhuman, the sacred boundary of the social sciences, is less interesting than the gradient of delegation, which ranges from the complete moral human being to the efficient machine. We tend to regard technology as only coming in at one end of the gradient, but what is remarkable about the engineer is that s/he can move up and down the gradient substituting one type of delegation for another. All of these forms of delegation incorporate the morality the engineer wishes to enforce.

To summarise, these two papers – one on scallops and fishermen and one on door-closers – offer us a remarkable way of understanding the construction of science and technology. Callon and Latour refuse to approach humans, nonhumans, nature, society as different a priori. They suggest a completely new form of social science which reintegrates nature and nonhumans into knowledge and networks. As Latour suggests, in the nineteenth century the masses forced their way into sociology; perhaps the end of the twentieth century will see nonhumans force their way into sociology. In general sociological terms, this approach is a marked departure from asymmetrical, determinist ventures. Callon and Latour ask us to see how interpretations emerge from networks, rather than assuming that we know in advance how networks are structured.

In terms of what we have seen so far, they advise us to extend our analyses beyond a social determinism. If we look at the account of gravity waves, for example, the only way a social determinist approach can come to understand the closure of the controversy is in terms of one actor crushing another. The controversy is played out in terms of social factors and excludes natural factors. We can imagine social class, or status, or power determining which view is ultimately successful. However, for Callon and Latour, we need to examine how a network of knowledge and actors is put together, how faithful the actors are to their representatives, how far the *interessement* devices work and how far the actors are enrolled, that is, accept the descriptions that are given to them. These networks are not just social, however, but are also natural.

In the next section, we examine the construction of scientific authority beyond particular science communities, in situations where we might expect the social processes of control, access, negotiation, and so on, to be more fluid and less well-defined. In particular, we consider the ways in which science integrates itself into wider social and cultural contexts, particularly policy contexts.

The next exercise will help you summarise what we've just covered.

EXERCISE 4.3

Okay, now it's time for you to help Devon out. He's about to burst in on Dermot yet again and, as you can expect, he's about to get another serve of Dermot's wit. We already know that Devon has worked his way through the material about reflexivity, about scallops and fishermen, and about door-closers. We also know that he did it in less than a positive spirit. You can imagine his next exchange with Dermot. At least we hope you can, as that's what we're asking you to do for this exercise.

Please write some dialogue for the next exchange between Devon and Dermot, as Devon tries to come to grips with the package of points about reflexivity, scallops, fishermen and door-closers. Do your best to build in at least five of the following summary points from that material:

- Social scientific knowledge about science is itself as subject to the processes of social construction and negotiation as the scientific knowledge it targets.
- This type of reflexivity is not the same thing as extreme relativism. The Pyrrhonian idea that we cannot even know that we cannot know anything makes this type of reflexivity a sort of 'relativist relativism'.
- If sociologists of science adopt a position of social realism, they miss much about the active process which is scientific discovery as they wait for 'scientific truth' to do its work.
- The role of nonhumans as actors in science needs to be understood, though it should be neither downplayed nor exaggerated.
- We should abandon all a priori distinctions between natural and social events and treat divisions between nature and society, between nonhumans and humans, as the *results* of networks rather than their starting points.
- In the story of the fishermen and the scallops, the researchers attempted to make the network (of knowledge and actors) as strong as possible by the process of *interessement*, the act of attempting to stabilise the identity of another actant by stabilising one's own links with that entity and weakening the links the entity has with other entities.
- *Interessement* does not always work; actants do not always accept the roles that are constructed for them. In this example, the enrolments involved were not accepted. The scallops refused to anchor, and some fishermen could not resist fishing the stocks the researchers built up. The scallops' abilities to anchor were now cast into doubt; the fishermen's desire to see the long-term restocking of the Bay was likewise now a dubious proposition. In this case, social and natural phenomena were reorganised in the same way.
- Callon does not rely on a 'sociological' explanation of what is true; rather he prefers to follow a social and natural network through to see how what is true is put together.
- Latour's account of the development of the automatic door-closer – the way feelings and desires are, literally, incorporated into this nonhuman delegate such that it incorporates the injunction to keep the door closed and still incorporates the possibility to get more complex, such that it might open doors as you approach, ask you to prove your identity, shut in dangerous situations, etc. – shows us the ways in which the distinction between human and

nonhuman, the sacred boundary of the social sciences, is less interesting than the gradient of delegation, which ranges from the complete moral human being to the efficient machine.
• In refusing to differentiate between humans and nonhumans or between nature and society a priori, Latour and Callon's examples suggest a completely new form of sociology which reintegrates nature and nonhumans into knowledge and networks. They ask us to see how interpretations emerge from networks, rather than assuming that we know in advance how networks are structured, assuming that we know how society works.

Science and policy

While it is usual to understand science as a value-free entity, used or misused in the public sphere, we have already seen how scientific fact is actively constructed by actors as much as by nature. Therefore, it is hardly surprising that what is to count as a scientific fact will include what we might term *values*. As Schwarz and Thompson (1990) argue, different protagonists in a scientific debate always have different ideas about what counts as a fact, and some negotiation has always to take place. Let's look at this more closely, using an example taken from their book.

A multinational corporation recently launched a lavatory rim-block which used paradichlorobenzene to make the perfumes and detergents operate together. The result sold like hot cakes (and to prove the point, a child actually ate one). Suddenly, an attack by the German Greens threw the situation into confusion. The Greens maintained that paradichlorobenzene is toxic and non-biodegradable and should not be introduced into the water supply. The multinational was dubious about the claim, but withdrew the product anyway. Three months later it had a new product. As it put it:

> The product was actually a better product in terms of perfume delivery and product life – a less expensive product and a new process with higher production capability. Armed with this the German launch went from strength to strength. We are now allowing the UK housewife to enjoy some of the benefits of our research efforts. (quoted in Schwarz and Thompson 1990: 3)

The initial problem here is that there were competing certainties as to what counted as a scientific fact. The Greens, seeing nature as perennially vulnerable, placed the burden of proof on those who wished to innovate. The slightest doubt about the toxicity or biodegradability of paradichlorobenzene meant that it needed to be removed from the market. The multinational was also concerned to protect the environment, but it regarded nature as more robust. It was happy to introduce new materials into the ecosystem once standard toxicity testing had taken place.

Another common-sense idea is that science policy is entirely determined by interests. This position suggests that science policy actors have pre-existing political interests which inform how they deal with science and technology. The weakness of this perspective is that it assumes that everyone knows in advance what they want and how they are going to get it. It denies the possibility that interests and technologies may mutually shape each other. To return to the lavatory rim-blocks example, an interests model would not account for the way in which the actors entered into the technology and transformed it such that it gave them rather more of what they liked about it and rather less of what they disliked about it.

Often in science policy disputes, then, it is not simply the case that there are two sides, one which favours a technology and the other which opposes it. More often what we see are ongoing attempts to reshape science and technology which then, in turn, reshape politics. To take this point further, we cannot assume that 'sides' are formed in advance of any scientific or technological controversy. It may well be that they are as much a construction as the science itself. We cannot assume interests, especially political interests, to be a priori and determining of techno-scientific development and of policy implementation. We have seen something of this approach in the actor-network theory of Callon and Latour – the formation of a techno-science network *includes* the construction of the interests and identities of the actors.

The basic point here is that the formation of science policy is a dynamic matter: we cannot straightforwardly read interests onto policy directions. For example, the 'war on cancer' was an idea which arose outside of scientific research circles and was originally opposed by many scientists. Nonetheless, the pressure groups which supported this initiative have convinced authorities to fund such projects and have enrolled many scientists to this point of view. Likewise, gay groups enrolled scientists to pay attention to AIDS. And in research into Alzheimer's Disease, the National Institute on Aging in the USA at first favoured basic research, but eventually built service research into its agenda as well.

In these last three examples, as well as in the rim-block example, the various protagonists engaged in a mutually transforming relationship with science and technology. In short, what we are suggesting here is that there may be some mileage in trying to understand the ways in which actors come to be associated with each other and coordinate their actions.

Let's look at Star and Griesemer's (1989) account of the funding and building of a new museum at the University of California. In their account, actors from very different social worlds cooperated to get the museum up and running. The various actors were the university administrators, who wanted to make the university a national-class establishment, amateur collectors, who wanted to collect and conserve California's flora and fauna, professional trappers, who wanted skins and furs to earn money, farmers, who served as occasional field-workers, and two individuals – Alexander, who was interested in conservation and education, and Grinnell, who wanted to demonstrate a theory that changing environments are the driving force behind evolution. Star and Griesemer suggest that cooperation between these different groups happened through the medium of what they term 'boundary objects':

> [Boundary objects] both inhabit several intersecting worlds . . . and satisfy the informational requirements of each of them. Boundary objects are objects which are both plastic enough to adapt to local needs and constraints of the several parties employing them, yet robust enough to maintain a common identity across sites. . . . They have different meanings in different social worlds but their structure is common enough to more than one world to make them recognizable, a means of translation. (1989: 393)

A boundary object permits the different groups to interact. It includes things like the museum itself as a repository, California and the standardised forms which Grinnell made for the trappers and amateur collectors to fill out. These boundary objects only emerged as the different groups met; they were not engineered by any one individual or group. Each of the boundary objects had a different meaning for the various actors, but the gradually emerging boundary objects slowly facilitated the construction of a network of actors. Within this network, the interests of the different actors became subtly transformed – one might even say constructed – as the network proceeded.

How does science turn into policy? It is important to note that there cannot be a privileged role for 'real scientists' or for 'true knowledge' in terms of a policy formulation. This cannot be so for a variety of reasons. There is usually a dispute as to what is true knowledge: in the lavatory-block example, there was a dispute over the effects of paradichlorobenzene; in debates over nuclear power or acid rain, scientists' knowledge is not absolute, but is always potentially challengeable. If you add to this the well-known phenomenon that pressure groups educate themselves in relevant scientific knowledge to compete on the same terrain with scientists (for example, cancer war proponents took on the cancer experts on their own expert-knowledge base), it should be clear that it is not possible for a 'true' science to dictate policy. So we can dispose of scientific or technological determinism as an explanation of how a policy might emerge.

However, we must also dispose of social determinism. We have seen that it is not enough to argue that dominant interests win out, because this suggests that interests are static and that they do not enter into the formation of science and technology. In fact, in the examples we have looked at, interests are actually shaped as part of an ongoing, dynamic network of actors. This is not to deny that actors bring interests with them to the networks, but it is to question the idea that these interests are calcified.

Perhaps the best way to think about the relation between science and policy is to consider the media of association and coordination that allow a policy to emerge. In doing this, we can make use of Callon and Latour's actor-network theory, but we might also consider the boundary objects which allow translations to occur between different actors.

Putting the science in society

We have already noted how any scientific fact must be spread further than the scientist or the laboratory if it is to have any power or status as a truth. Scientific knowledge, then, must move into a more public sphere if it is to triumph. We can extend this by thinking about the use of the public experiment. As Collins (1988) points out, the public experiment – a demonstration of a scientific truth – is a paradoxical endeavour. Proximity usually leads to uncertainty; it is distance that leads to certainty about a scientific truth. Basically, when one is close to a scientific experiment, one can see the fallibility, the manipulation, the skill – in short, the social negotiation of the experiment. The paradox of the public experiment is that it brings those who are to be convinced uncomfortably close to science and risks allowing them to see that the truth is not so clear-cut. In fact, Collins argues (1987, 1988), our distance from science-in-the-making is the source of any certainty that we might have. Another paradox involved here is that the general public is presumed to be able to form a conclusion on the basis of matters that are not even agreed upon by the 'experts'.

The use of a public experiment or demonstration has a long history. As Shapin (1988) points out, even by the mid-seventeenth century there was a distinction made between trying an experiment and showing it. The trying phase was a private arrangement whereby the scientist would try to make the thing work. This corresponds to something like research proper. The showing phase was conducted in the public sphere, and was the demonstration of something that you had practised and made to work. As Shapin puts it, 'The career of experimental knowledge is the circulation between private and public spaces' (1988: 375). Similarly, Gooding (1985) describes the distinction between experiment and demonstration in the work of Faraday in the nineteenth century. Faraday practised his experiments in the basement of the Royal Institution. When they worked, he would bring them up to the lecture theatre on the first floor to demonstrate each novel effect. As Gooding puts it, you can trace the careers of natural phenomena from their tentative existence and inception in the basement, until they made it up to the first floor as a fact.

Now these distinctions still may be valid today, but as Collins notes (1988: 730), nowadays broadcast media allow everyone to be the audience of a demonstration. Why, you might ask, do scientists bother with displays that attempt to popularise their findings? As we already know, a finding gains strength by being seen outside the laboratory. In the seventeenth century scientists would routinely perform their experiments in the houses of gentlemen. These gentlemen could vouch for the scientific claim on the basis of their position in society. Modern displays of science continue this tradition, although of course the audience has become more popular.

If we return to the initial paradoxes noted by Collins, we can begin to see how these are overcome. First of all, the audience is rarely allowed to see science first-hand; it is shown an edited, cleaned-up version – a demonstration rather than an experiment. In addition, when the public audience is shown science through the medium of, say, television, it gets to see a science which is nicely edited by the producers; science comes without all the cock-ups and the boring preparation. The public, then, is not really allowed to see science 'up close' – the distance that allows for certainty is preserved. Second, the public is presented with a demonstration which does not really allow a questioning of outcomes, or at least not without a huge technical knowledge which the audience does not have. Any disagreements between experts over what the demonstration might mean are pretty much glossed over. In this way, the lay audience is made more certain of its knowledge than the experts can ever be.

To take a concrete example, Collins (1988) reports a public experiment made by the British Central Electricity Generating Board (CEGB). The CEGB transported used nuclear fuel, sealed in special flasks, by rail to a central facility for reprocessing. This transportation aroused some concern because it was thought that the flasks might break open in the event of an accident. The CEGB arranged a public demonstration in which a train travelling at 100 miles per hour crashed into a flask. The idea was to show that the flask would not open even in these extreme conditions. The demonstration was a success, in that the flask did not break open. The public could now believe that the transportation of spent nuclear fuel was safe, because the containers were shown to be indestructible.

However, Greenpeace had a very different reading of this demonstration. Their spokespeople argued that conditions were organised such as to favour the survival of the flask. Greenpeace pointed out that the flask was thicker and more resilient than the standard flask and suggested scenarios which would be more damaging for the flask (for example, falling onto rock from a high bridge). They also claimed that the locomotive used in the test was a 'soft-nose' variety, which would do less damage than many other locomotives used by British Rail.

The point here is that the public was shielded from all this controversy in the demonstration. In a real experiment, there would be argument over what the results meant; but in the demonstration the results were arranged beforehand. It's a bit like at school when one is taught science through what appear to be experiments but are really pre-arranged displays (which are often botched; the schoolchild usually doesn't have the technical nous to dispute them). Collins suggests that it is not better education of the technicalities of science that would aid public understanding of science, rather it is a better understanding of the difference between an experiment and a demonstration, and a better understanding of how science is made.

This is something of a hot issue, given just how much the coverage of science has increased since the 1980s (Fayard 1993). Science journalism, which originated between the world wars (Lewenstein 1995), is now the place where this type of demonstration of science takes place. What we need to remember about this type of reporting is that it favours a particular model of science. As Nelkin (1987) has shown, science journalists tend to have a commitment to scientific values, rather than those of the public they are meant to inform. As a result, their reporting is likely to give a picture of science as a coherent body of knowledge about a natural reality, produced by careful methods.

It is a mistake to regard real science as taking place in the laboratory and equally a mistake to regard the popularisation of that science as being what goes on outside the laboratory. As Latour (1988) explains in relation to Pasteur's work on inoculation, Pasteur had to translate the findings of his laboratory into real situations involving anthrax, cattle, poultry, and so on. As we have already seen, in actor-network theory the production of scientific truths depends upon the construction of a network in which a whole series of identities have been stabilised. One of the ways scientists attempt to translate their findings and get a wider audience to back them up is by the use of modified scientific settings, particularly scientific demonstrations. The demonstration is a carefully calibrated version of the pure research. In the modern age, the role of demonstration has fallen also to journalists and television documentary makers, but their vision of science is one which perhaps makes it difficult for the public to appreciate how science is made.

In the next exercise, we'd like you to think about the wider context within which science takes place.

EXERCISE 4.4

Invent your own scientific experiment and use it as the basis to build your own account (about 1,000 words) of science at work in a social setting, complete of course with science policy and a science-hungry media. Here's a list of actors, taken from the above discussion, some of which you might like to build into the network(s) of your example (though of course you should feel free to invent your own actors): lavatory rim-blocks, chemicals, Green parties, the market, the public, scientific research institutes, gay groups, the National Institute on Aging, the University of California Museum, university administrators, amateur collectors, professional trappers, the Royal Institution, television science programmes, other science media, the British Central Electricity Generating Board, Greenpeace, special flasks, British Rail, school science classes.

   As you write, please try to make use of some of the points made in our above discussion.

'Right, I've dealt with Foucault, I've dealt with Latour and Callon, I've even dealt with their scallops and door-closers. I know about how science policy is constructed and how science is popularised. Now I'm ready for new challenges. Cathy says she's going to a new seminar on Foucault as a theorist of popular culture. After all this science malarky, that should be a breeze. What say we go along?'

Devon was bubbling with enthusiasm and confidence – a rare sight. How would Dermot respond?

'Can you reach the volume control, Dev? I can hardly hear it.'

5

'Can I apply this stuff to Shakespeare and shopping?'

CONTENTS

'Oh yeah, high five me baby! I've got Foucault down, Latourian twist and all,' Eric bragged in a poor imitation of the George and Kramer characters on Seinfeld (he didn't even know he was mixing them up).

Meryl was in celebratory mood too, so she wasn't going to tell him his imitation stank. Like Eric, she was thrilled to bits at her final grade in the Social Research Methods course. She too had taken a big risk in choosing to tackle the Foucault option and we all know the thrill available when a risky course of action reaps big rewards. Some of us, though, also know the ensuing enthusiasm can sometimes go too far. Yes, Meryl and Eric are in for a fall.

'What will we accomplish next?' Meryl replied, in a tone calculated to keep the bubbles flowing and in such a way as to allow her to answer her own question without a pause. 'Let's hammer that Cultural Studies course and make Michel and Bruno sing popular culture for us.'

'Nice one baby!' Eric was the sort to stick to a line of supposed humour until the corpse was rotting. 'We can apply what we know – and ain't that everything?

*– to TV, movies, novels, plays, shopping, sport, dancing, music. . . . Wow, where
will it end, baby?'*

*Well, we think it'll end in tears. It's going to take us all of this chapter to set
out our case against the step Eric and Meryl are already shuffling to. We're bound
to bore you more than they would, though we hope you bear with us while we
mess up their fun – we know we're right, but we'll try to keep our sancti-
moniousness to a minimum. We'll spend a little time (not too much) showing you
why the Foucaultian methods we've detailed in the book so far are not the sort of
methods you can simply 'apply' to diverse cultural objects like a coat of paint.
After this, we'll show you how a very different, much more subtle approach to
culture is available using Foucault's methods. We do this by taking you back to
school – via an extended discussion of schooling as culture. If slogans help you
along in learning your methods, a good one here is: 'Foucault's methods give us
a cultural studies much more about managing than meaning.'*

Cultural studies as studies of meanings – Foucault's methods don't belong here

An extreme example of cultural studies as studies of meaning is provided
by the American humourist Robert Benchley. In a piece from much earlier
this century he parodies this type of analysis. He first offers a brief snippet
of Shakespeare, riddled with footnote markers:

> Enter first Lady-in-Waiting (Flourish,[1] Hautboys[2] and[3] torches[4]).
> First Lady-in-Waiting – What[5] ho![6] Where[7] is[8] the[9] music?[10] (1937: 235)

He then offers a set of notes for the ten markers. Included are:

2. *Hautboys*, from the French *haut*, meaning 'high' and the Eng. *boys*, meaning
   'boys'. The word here is doubtless used in the sense of 'high boys', indicat-
   ing either that Shakespeare intended to convey the idea of spiritual distress
   on the part of the First Lady-in-Waiting or that he did not.
3. *and*. A favourite conjunctive of Shakespeare's in referring to the need for a
   more adequate navy for England. Tauchnitz claims that it should be pro-
   nounced 'und', stressing the anti-penult. This interpretation, however, has
   found disfavour among most commentators because of its limited significance. (1937: 236)

Benchley concludes his sketch:

> The meaning of the whole passage seems to be that the First Lady-in-Waiting
> has entered, concomitant with a flourish, hautboys and torches and says, 'What
> ho! Where is the music?' (1937: 238)

Of course we wouldn't be so cruel as to suggest that Foucaultian scholars
of cultural objects could be so obsessed with meaning that they would leave
themselves open to this sort of parody. If only. Here's just two sentences

from the preface to a recent (1997) special issue of a cultural studies journal dedicated to Foucaultian thinking:

> This journal aims for the communication of world thinkings. World thinkings use the force of thought that seeks in the temporal domain to overcome the *fin-de-siècle* transition from the twentieth to the twenty-first century, to serve in the spatial domain as a vitalizing force for a diversity of place-existence pratiques that escape the comprehension of simultaneous thinking on a global scale. (Yamamoto 1997: 3)

Such high-falutin theorising is not really our concern here. All we're aiming to do, as we suggested above, is quickly show what can go wrong when students get it into their heads that Foucault's methods are like those do-it-yourself wall-filler products that promise certain results if you just 'aim and squirt', at whatever surface you care to pick. As with home maintenance, such short-cut uses of Foucault's methods in regard to various cultural objects turn out to be at best disappointing and at worst disastrous. Just as the short-cut wall-fillers turn out not to work unless you've done some proper preparation not mentioned in the ads, so with the short-cut uses of Foucault's methods. Let's rejoin Eric and Meryl to see what we mean.

In their Cultural Studies class, they've just dealt with some work by Stuart Hall, one of the world's best known and most respected cultural studies scholars. In many books and articles across a long period his work has come to be synonymous with an accessible, sensible, careful approach to the study of culture. In more recent years Hall has, like so many scholars, become convinced of the worth of Foucault's methods. From his seminal essay 'Cultural Studies: Two Paradigms' (1980) through to later studies of British culture under Margaret Thatcher (for example 1988a, 1988b, 1988c), Hall has sought to import Foucault into the cultural studies tradition. Unfortunately he never goes so far as to use Foucault to question the assumptions of meaning-search. He encourages his readers to drag Foucault under the 'deep' water of 'deep' meaning, that is, to try to make him simply another resource in the study of culture as the site where hegemonic and resistant meanings ritually (and endlessly) do battle. For example, in the 'Two Paradigms' essay we find the exhortation that Foucault's 'general epistemological position' not be 'swallowed whole', on the grounds that Foucault is 'deeply committed to the necessary non-correspondence of all practices to one another' and as such is no help in the theorisation of 'the social formation' (1980: 71).

Even more pointed are some comments in one of his essays on Thatcherite culture. Here he recruits Foucault to help polish the tarnished concept of ideology, the very concept Foucault so pointedly rejects. Hall writes in praise of Foucault's 'development of the analysis of *the discursive*' as something which 'necessarily modifies, in a radical way, the traditional material/ideal, base/superstructure dichotomies of classical marxist theories of ideology' (1988b: 51, emphasis in original). For Hall, Foucault can thus help us confirm that '[n]o social practice exists outside of the domain of the semiotic – the practices and production of meaning' (1988b: 51).

In short, Hall does not treat Foucault seriously, using him only up to the point where he might frighten the children – that is, up to the point where he might disturb the obviousness of culture as meaning. Of course, for us, a Foucault that does not disturb the obviousness of something is no Foucault at all. To take another example, we can only be disappointed, to say the least, that in one of his other pieces on Thatcherite culture, Hall follows a ringing endorsement of Foucault's handling of power – 'Power is never merely repressive but, in Foucault's sense, always productive' (Hall 1988a: 3) – with an account seemingly devoid of this insight. For the rest of this piece, power is conceptualised as the possession of powerful figures, in a very un-Foucaultian manner. Culture here remains a repository of those meanings accepted and promoted by the powerful, in this case, Margaret Thatcher and the Thatcherites. The suggestion is that most Brits could not escape these meanings and so took them on as their own. The concept of power is used only as a synonym for membership of the board of the Culture Meaning-Bank – the powerful help stock the bank with those meanings which suit them; the powerless have no choice but to withdraw these meanings and eventually come to accept them as their own.

Of course, while we hear Hall's words as the sound of Foucault spinning in his grave, Eric and Meryl hear them as the starting gun in a race to slap Foucault's methods on as many cultural objects as possible.

'Oh baby, we're really getting somewhere now! Foucault and Latour helping us to tell people how things really are. What could be better!'

Eric was full of himself after only a couple of classes in the new Cultural Studies course. Meryl was hardly any more humble. They even turned up at a Cultural Studies conference nearby to hear the Foucaultian contributions. Unfortunately they were not disappointed. They attended a paper on the shopping mall as panopticon and another which argued that modern gymnasia, with mirrors everywhere, are disciplinary mechanisms for producing docile bodies: examples of Foucault's work being wildly over-generalised and applied in a glue-on fashion to diverse cultural objects.

We need to take a little more time to further outline the problem involved here. If you're interested in consumption, for example (shopping and so on, not tuberculosis), you might reasonably ask why you cannot borrow from *Discipline and Punish* a few facts about the modern docile and disciplined individual and apply them to users of shopping malls. The point to remember is that Foucault's books are specific histories of specific objects, not recipes for those interested in (half-)baking accounts of the meaning of modern life. Don't forget the historical work is *problem-based*; so a new problem will certainly throw up a new historical account. The historical account of *Discipline and Punish* cannot be carelessly used again and again. This point brings us to an important observation: that Foucault's work does not allow us to reach general conclusions about the content of modern life – the point is to show precisely how some event has its own specificity (and here we refer you back to our earlier discussion of the contrast between total and general histories).

This misunderstanding is the source of the oft-repeated criticisms of Foucault that his methods do not take enough account of religion, or gender, or class, or resistance, or whatever the particular critic thinks is important (see Leonard 1980; Taylor 1985; Sawicki 1991). Foucault is not telling us that power is important to our society, or that discipline is everywhere. Rather, these concepts emerge out of his work on the birth of specific modern objects. We should neither latch on to Foucault's concepts as analytical panacea, nor suggest alternative ones that are more likely to fill this role; we need, rather, to use history carefully, in the manner we outlined in Chapters 1 and 2, to deal with only our own area of investigation.

As we said, we think the main thing we have to get across to Eric and Meryl and others in their position, to lead them away from the pitfalls of the culture-as-meaning approach, is the possibility of seeing culture as management or administration. Before we turn to that task, however, we should add that this proposed rescue vehicle is not the only one available for good Foucaultian scholars. We think it's the best one available, but we are only too keen to acknowledge the strides made by good Foucaultian scholars in using Foucault to tackle cultural objects head on.

Simon During's work, for example, shows us how Foucault's methods can be used to help study literature. During unpacks the various themes of Foucault's research and then uses only those that are historically relevant to discuss particular pieces of literature. For instance, he carefully borrows from Foucault's work on medicine the way in which people could understand themselves in relation to death, and then shows how this conceptualisation can be applied to *Madame Bovary* or *Middlemarch*.

> Whereas in *Madame Bovary* death represents a limit, a finitude; here it is everywhere in the form of decay and individual and social pathology. Whereas *Madame Bovary* presents its readers with a detailed, clinical description of death that has no utilitarian or ethical function, in *Middlemarch* the pure gaze has been replaced by a surveillance of the living which can only treat of things and events that have a capacity for exchange, or tend towards the status of information. In *Middlemarch*, characters are, to various degrees, either on the side of life (and energy) or approaching death (and repetition/stasis). (During 1992: 62)

Unlike Hall's approach, this opens up possibilities for looking at old topics in new ways, especially as During is aware of the danger of treating Foucault's work as a yardstick for any other area of inquiry. And, we should stress in closing this discussion, During is not alone in this achievement; Toby Miller (1993) provides an equally careful use of Foucault's methods in regard to certain cultural objects, most notably the 'well-tempered self'.

Now we'd like you to think some more about how Foucault's careful work can be carelessly applied.

EXERCISE 5.1

From at least a glance at *Discipline and Punish* (we hope you'll read it all), make a list of three or more points that could easily be the source of over-generalisations about culture, if handled carelessly. Now use these over-generalisations to plan an account of a well-known cultural object – television for example. What sort of account of the function of television in modern society are you likely to produce? What are the problems of such an account?

Please write about 1,000 words.

(What we hope you gain from this exercise is the insight – unfortunately not one shared by all cultural studies commentators – that the television and any of Foucault's objects, say the prison, have very different histories and social functions, that glib accounts of similarities should be treated with suspicion.)

Now we must begin the task of convincing Eric and Meryl.

Cultural studies as studies of management – Foucault's methods right at home

As we noted in the introduction to this chapter, we aim here to take you on a ride through an extended discussion of schooling, to show you schooling as a place where Foucault's methods can be used to deal with culture in a way substantially different to the 'search for meanings' approach outlined and rejected above.

Foucault and schooling as a site of culture

For more than twenty years Foucaultian scholarship in the history of education has attempted to transform understandings of the birth and contemporary character of the classroom. Foucault himself devoted a large part of his *Discipline and Punish* (1977) to a description of the way a specifically modern form of individuality was built using new forms of architecture, new organisations of time and space, and new ways of distributing and ordering bodies. What methodological principles can we glean from this approach when we start to think about education?

Most analyses of the development of popular education from the end of the eighteenth century stressed the (successful or flawed) realisation of a set of principles or ideas. Typically, liberals are convinced that the school was and is a breeding ground for a collective rationality (Gutmann 1987) and Marxists that the school was and is an instrument of class rule (Bowles and Gintis 1976; Willis 1977). We can deal in a little more detail with Marxist approaches. For these critics of the education system, the school is an unmitigated disaster. For example, it can be understood as the breeding ground for a new batch of disciplined and docile working-class kids. Willis's approach is a good example of this kind of thinking, an approach which takes a great deal from Althusser's theory of ideology (see especially Althusser 1971). For Althusser, the education system is the crucial locale for the reproduction of society, complete with ruling-class ideology. Educational settings allow for the maintenance of the status quo. Schools, by teaching certain skills, certain forms of comportment (like conscientiousness or good manners), provide the practical 'know-how' that enables capitalism to survive and develop.

An alternative version is also sometimes espoused, which views the working class as central to the development of their own education in that they are meant to be the catalysts for it (see, for example, Bowles and Gintis 1976). For this Marxist approach, the school is perhaps a different kind of disaster – a disaster of failed possibilities.

A distinctively Foucaultian approach to questions in the history of education has emerged which has challenged these positions. As early as 1979, Jones and Williamson produced an essay which stresses how compulsory schooling in the nineteenth century emerged out of a series of concerns with crime, poverty and international competitiveness – concerns which had been quickly and to some extent fortuitously rendered practicable by the collection of a body of statistical knowledge about cities, towns and their inhabitants. Jones and Williamson, using Foucault's methods very carefully, describe the emergence of a new interventionist strategy, given sudden urgency by the formation of new knowledge about the population. Like Foucault's, their analysis deliberately avoids reducing the complexity of historical change to simple stories of cause and effect, or of exaggerating the importance of a set of local and contingent events by giving them an overarching logic or meaning.

Hunter's later analysis (1994) of the school complements Jones and Williamson's (1979). Hunter argues that the modern school is the product of, on the one hand, the determinedly secular desires of the bureaucratic and administrative state to train its population, and, on the other, the adaptation of Christian pastoral techniques – techniques of spiritual discipline. For Hunter, the modern school aims at the formation of individuals who can be self-reflective and self-governing. Once again, Hunter's work suggests that the development of a recognisably modern education system is much less systematic and less 'meaningful' than it appears or than its critics have suggested.

We can already see the different picture of culture involved in using Foucault's methods in this way – culture as a set of (governmental and other) practices aimed at producing certain sorts of persons, not as a collection of phenomena which hold meanings like a bank, from which people withdraw and to which they deposit.

The school, for this Foucaultian approach, is an amalgam of the limited practical resources that educationalists are able to put to use to try to deal with limited, local problems. Hoskin (1993) also stresses the lack of any

overarching logic or meaning in dealing with the rise of three fundamental educational knowledge-producing sites: the classroom, the
laboratory and the seminar, all at the end of the eighteenth century, but
at slightly different times and in different places (Scotland, France and
Germany, respectively), relating the emergence of all three to the widespread adoption of formal examinations, mathematical-style grading
and the use of writing by and about students as a replacement for a pre-
dominantly oral tradition. For Hoskin, discipline (as both administration
of individuals, including self-administration, and a system of knowledge) is something which emerged from the mundane practices of educational life – writing, examining, grading. Shifts in the way we 'learned
to learn' at the end of the eighteenth century provided an amazingly
fertile breeding ground for new forms of social and economic organisation and new forms of self. To expand on this somewhat: Hoskin
and Macve (1993) argue that the emergence of the modern business enterprise can be linked to such innovative educational establishments –
rather than to the practical demands of the industrial revolution (cf.
Chandler 1977).

It is worth reiterating some key points about the Foucaultian approach
used in this research into schooling as culture. First, it relies on the importance of chance in the history of the modern classroom. Out of a chaotic set
of possibilities for the organisation of popular education, modern forms
of schooling gradually came to take a shape that they still possess today.
As this ragbag of knowledge, practices and programmes was gradually
put together, new practices were invented and old practices were revitalised and pressed into service for new tasks.

Second, it allows us to see that the classroom did not emerge as an
attempt to foster the liberal, free, rational individual or as a result of the
working class's efforts to educate and politicise itself. From its beginnings
this type of schooling was profoundly bureaucratic and disciplinary,
rather than democratic or progressive-revolutionary – concerned with the
management of lives, not the meanings they drew on or left aside. On the
other hand, we cannot assume that the classroom is an instrument of
ruling-class political will, a technical means for imposing a lived ideology
on the helpless, crushed individualities of schoolchildren. For Jones and
Williamson, Hunter, and Hoskin, remember, the classroom was and is
fundamentally contingent, with dispersed beginnings and piecemeal
development.

Third, forms of self, modes of ethical comportment, ways of knowing
and of disciplining, are better thought of as products of the classroom
rather than pre-existing entities; culture produces persons, it does not
operate with and/or for pre-acculturated individuals. The classroom
should be thought of not as the site where the child is imperfectly liberated, but rather as the environment where children are positively constructed within specific institutional forms. The modern classroom is
above all an arena which is productive of specific, historically localised

forms of subjectivity; it is not a site for fostering a priori rational individuals, nor a site for the repression and denial of true individuality.

The Foucaultian work discussed in this section, as is to be expected with this use of Foucault's methods, and as we have been at pains to stress throughout the book, gives us a rather 'flat' description of these historical events because it deliberately eschews recourse to 'deeper' explanations of education (such as theories of 'the hidden curriculum') or deeper meanings of the self. Educational innovation, for Foucaultians of our stamp, is not the creature of systematic social, economic or political change and the schoolchild is not a bastardised or bowdlerised version of the 'true' self, a betrayal of what could have been and an obstacle to what should be – some artefact of 'genuine' culture. The classroom, then, might be considered as a cautiously 'experimental' response to historically located problems of the moral training of the population. What we are suggesting here is that as a cultural institution (in our sense of that term), the classroom was born as an experiment, in two ways: first, in that it was a hopeful attempt to deal with a specific set of problems of moral training; second, in that it emerged from a tradition which was closely connected to 'science'. We argue that the contemporary classroom bears the marks of these origins, remaining fundamentally bureaucratic and yet experimental, a modern product of a knowledge complex, simultaneously political, economic and psychological.

'Oh yeah, I think I see where this is going,' Eric postured to Meryl. 'Schools are part of culture because the discourse of schooling helps kids become ideologically saturated by the dominant culture.'

Meryl was suddenly not so confident. She is a bit quicker on the uptake than Eric and could sense that the new material they were now coming across was different from the cultural studies stuff they were becoming used to, and different in more than just style. She wasn't sure enough of her ground at this stage to do any more than sense an obstacle to their plan to make Foucault and Latour belt out the tunes of standard cultural studies, but even this pause by Meryl was enough to at least temper Eric's gung-ho attitude.

'Let's push on a bit with this schooling stuff before we say that for sure,' she counselled, this time in a tone calculated to let Eric know she wasn't joking.

'Okay,' he said, without really meaning it and trying hard to hide his disappointment that suddenly he wasn't the leader of a fearless band of two, determined to make Foucault's methods exactly the same as existing cultural studies methods.

He didn't hide it well, but Meryl decided that now wasn't the time to tell him so. They both let it ride, but both knew that the friendship they'd forged on the basis of their joint foray into cultural studies had taken an irreversible turn, as indeed had their foray. Things were about to get worse for them.

The complexity of the classroom as culture: science, economics, morals, administration   The classroom was invented as a cautious experiment, as we said

earlier, and remains an experimental space in that a whole series of experimental strategies, dreams, programmes, and so forth, are brought to bear
and tested there; yet these experiments are always productive in the sense
that ideas, objects, actors, new forms of self, emerge from this arena.

The science studies approach which featured heavily in the two previous
chapters includes work that argues both that the laboratory resembles the
factory and that the factory resembles the laboratory (see, for example,
Miller and O'Leary 1994). The laboratory is a site for the *manufacture* of
ideas, objects and actors and can thus be seen as factory-like (Latour and
Woolgar 1986; Hacking 1992b), while the factory is a place of closely controlled experimentation and can thus be seen as laboratory-like:

> For the factory is as much a site of invention and intervention as the laboratory
> populated by physicists, chemists, and the like. This is self-evident for the prod-
> ucts made in the factory. But the factory is a site for invention and intervention
> in a further important sense. It is here, on the shop floor, that new realities are
> created out of the dreams and schemes of diverse agents and experts based in a
> multiplicity of locales. The rearranging of persons and things on the factory floor
> ... customer-driven manufacturing, and designs for the 'Factory of the Future'
> have made the factory in the laboratory par excellence. Out of such interven-
> tions have emerged new physical spaces on the shop floor, new ways of calcu-
> lating, new forms of work organization, and new modes of economic
> citizenship.... As such, the factory is an intrinsically theoretical and experi-
> mental space, one where phenomena are created. (Miller and O'Leary 1994: 470)

Our primary concern here is with the contemporary classroom as implicated in the production of 'culture' and cultural values, with the 'installa-
tion' of culture in young children, that is, with the ways the classroom is
connected to practices which allow the child to internalise culture-as-
management. There has been much important work done recently which
has fruitfully examined these questions (see, for example, Corrigan and
Sayer 1985; Hunter 1989, 1994; Donald 1992), but these studies only deal in
passing, if at all, with what we take to be the two fundamental characteristics of the modern classroom alluded to above: it is modelled on the
laboratory as an 'experimental space' and it resembles the factory inasmuch
as it needs an 'output' or 'manufacture'. What might such a claim mean?

The classroom can be thought of as a space where a whole series of experimental strategies, dreams, programmes, and so forth, are brought to bear
and tested out. Yet these experiments are always productive in the sense that
ideas, objects, actors and inscriptions emerge from this arena. These productions provide a functional justification for the classroom. All that Miller
and O'Leary claim for the factory–laboratory can be claimed, *mutatis mutan-
dis*, for the classroom. In addition, it is possible to extend the factory
metaphor not just to the 'manufactures' of the classroom, but also to the way
in which processes like costing, teaching quality assessments and the rene-
gotiation of working practices have been inserted into education.

In this chapter we are offering an account that stems from a larger study of reading instruction techniques in two first-year infant classes at different schools in an English inner-city district. The children in these classes were aged four or five at the time of our study. The study includes material drawn from extended interviews with two teachers and field notes from participant observation.

We turn first to the role of the teacher in running the classroom as factory–laboratory. The modern classroom does not have a simple, transparent relation to the academic, educational and political discourses that attempt to shape it. The classroom has a certain independence, an autonomy partly given it by the fact that the teacher is constituted as the sovereign. A teacher remarks in response to an interview question, 'Each teacher is a queen of a very tiny area. I mean, I am in control here, I am the boss.' Later on, when one of the children in her classroom is indirectly quizzed about this by the interviewer, she confirms that, indeed, Ms Williamson is the boss.

If the teacher is in charge, this is not to say that his or her organisation of the classroom is predicated on subjective preference; teacher training, refresher courses, teachers' own self-help groups and in-service training courses all combine to ensure that the teacher is enmeshed in a complex of knowledge about control of the classroom. But contradictions in the methods teachers are taught, the teachers' own resistance to particular methods, and the acquisition of their own idiosyncratic tactics as a result of experience at the 'chalk-face' produce a series of heterogeneous practices which exhibit a 'relative autonomy'. All of which points to the rather 'hit-and-miss' nature of any strategic interventions aimed at the classroom. The transmission of culture through schooling, by this Foucaultian understanding of culture, is a fragile practice, so contingent that it is hard to pick out an overarching logic or state-inspired programme, for example.

Nonetheless, it is important to point to the ways in which educational and psychological knowledge have produced the teacher's understanding of his or her activities in the classroom. In particular, these different types of knowledge give the teacher a picture of the child as an active learner, with many of the skills required for reading and language acquisition latent within:

> Language, with its four elements of speaking, listening, reading and writing, cannot and should not be regarded as a subject to be taught. (*Language Policy and Guidelines* n.d.: 1)

A theorisation of a priori rule-systems, which are contained within the child's genetic make-up and which virtually pre-programme the child's learning, can be seen in perhaps the two most important theorists of child development and language acquisition, Piaget and Chomsky, and in most of the influential developmental psychological and educational theories which directly or indirectly build upon these thinkers (see especially Piaget 1959; Chomsky 1965).

Such notions of education and development unsurprisingly contain within them the possibility of understanding the teacher's role as facilitative rather than directly instructional (Walkerdine 1988). Even in the most 'social' of theories of child development and education, such as the Vygotskian or Meadian perspectives which stress the interaction between teacher and child, the crucial element is seen to be the child's internalisation of social processes. In this way, the social is quickly reduced to individual cognitive processes which can be sped up or retarded according to the appropriateness of the environment. Thus, even the most self-consciously interactive developmental and educational theories fall prey to the Kantian problem of the relation between the knower and the known. As with Kant's express duality of the knower and the known, these accounts rely on an a priori individual, a reductionism which requires an 'homunculus' to do the internalising (see Henriques et al. 1984).

By this account, the teacher is in charge of the classroom, but the fundamental natures of the substances and forces contained within that classroom are not alterable; processes may be helped or hindered by the teacher's activities, but his/her sphere of influence is strictly circumscribed since development is construed as internal to the child. Consequently, we might think of the teacher as something like a 'technician' within the specific field of operations that is the classroom. Experiments in changing the *modus operandi* of the classroom, such as the reorganisation of the position of desks from formal rows to informal 'islands' that accompanied the progressivism of the 1960s (Walkerdine 1984), can be seen as the manipulation of a variable within an experimental setting. Rather like the classical model of the relationship between the scientist and things in the laboratory, which we problematised, with much help from Latour and Callon, in the previous two chapters, the child and the teacher are cast in quite separate roles, with the reality and 'truth' of childhood located at a 'deep' level beyond the reach of the teacher. Manipulations in the experimental setting can facilitate the child's progress or militate against it, but only as a chemist's manipulation of the elements allows 'natural' combinations to occur and stand apart from the subjective interference of the technician or experimenter. Perhaps, just as this model of the scientist as the impartial observer and discloser of natural truths has lost prestige, so we may one day come to be disillusioned with developmental theories which locate development inside the child and theorise the social context as 'interference' or 'facilitation'.

Our Foucaultian picture of culture-as-management can be taken to surprising places. It can deal with the fact that one of the consequences of the above-described instrumental role for the teacher is a series of quite remarkable qualities and behaviours being linked to that role. For example, the teacher is required to 'love' his/her pupils equally; this specific form of love is a detached, platonic, calm surveillance of the classroom and its emotional problems. The teacher, then, has become a kind of 'pastor' of the children. Anxiety is the consequence of a failure to conduct this pastoral role well. For example, Ms McCarthy talks in the following terms of John, one of the children she does not particularly care for:

Really I should be trying to mother him a bit, but I can't stand it. It's awful, I hope I don't show it too much. . . . It does irritate me that. Yeah, and you can't help it so you've got to make a special effort with the ones you don't care for. The only thing that worries me, that relieves me I should say, is that I felt this way about him before I knew all that was going on. I think I'm going to have to work very hard and make a special effort.

Ms McCarthy refers to the recent discovery of a history of sexual abuse in the child's family; her anxiety at being unable to bring herself to 'love' the child, and her relief when she discovers there is a reason why this platonic and pure love has been disrupted are what are most noticeable in her frank remarks. The teacher here is clearly constituted as someone much more than the person who teaches reading, yet there is a reciprocal relationship between this pastoral care and good instruction; so, the teaching of reading is profoundly affected by the emotional dynamics of the classroom:

It . . . it is difficult. You just have to make sure you spend the same amount of time with them all, with their reading and everything. And I'm especially careful to spend the right amount of time with John, well because . . . well, you know.

How has the teacher's conduct become linked to such a pastoral role, and how is this connected to the factory–laboratory account of the classroom we are arguing for? The beginnings of an answer lie in investigating how the classroom is also connected to questions of citizenship. The path of culture-as-management is a complex one.

'I'm not so sure we can just say these teachers and kids are ideologically saturated by the dominant culture,' Meryl suggested as gently as she could. 'It seems a bit more complex than that.'

Eric's first reaction was to argue. 'But look at what they're saying. Surely all this guff about how to deal with the kids in the school is masking the fact that they're learning to fit in to the dominant culture, just like the teachers already do. I can even guess where these schools are and I'll bet the kids are going to end up either as shitkickers in a factory or on the dole.'

'Come on Eric, you're jumping to conclusions. You may be right about what's going to happen to them, but that doesn't mean the culture is as straightforward as we thought.'

Eric wasn't ready to give in straight away. 'I never thought it was straightforward. We haven't even factored in the way TV, movies, newspapers, fashion, music and lots of other things add to the meaning of schooling for these kids.' He felt chuffed as he said it.

Meryl wanted to argue with him but still wasn't sure enough of her ground. Maybe they were right before, she thought to herself. She decided to leave it for a while, though Eric's smugness bothered her.

So how would you deal with an essay on schooling?

EXERCISE 5.2

Please draw up a list of features of schooling in the late twentieth-century western world. Develop these features into a plan (about 700 words) for an essay which is consistent with our Foucaultian account of culture-as-management.

Producing citizens, installing culture The teacher, then, is responsible for the ambience of the classroom, the correct deployment of its resources; it must be something like a 'learning environment', but it is more than that – it is a place for the constitution of young, autonomous citizens. In this section we argue that the production of citizens is a fundamental concern of the classroom as culture. We also argue that this aim is an instance of the classroom both as factory (there is an obvious 'product') and as laboratory (a series of experiments have been instituted to help this productive process).

The teacher's love for the children is a technique for producing citizens, especially in those instances where the home does not provide the right sort of environment. Ms McCarthy continues to talk about the troublesome John:

> It's just as I say, you don't get that much help from the parents. I've only ever seen his mother once; now there's some man appeared called Malcolm, so I don't know what the mum's doing. She's supposed to be seeing the children but I don't know what she's doing.

The teacher cannot just pursue the simple business of teaching John to read; the family dynamics press in on her, she has a role to play in compensating a child who has now been placed in care. Although the interviewer made it explicit that he was interested in the children's instruction in reading, this is only one of many examples which shows that it is impossible to keep this domain separate from all the other parts of modern primary school pedagogy. The 'instruction' of the child is never quite enough, in terms of his or her 'education', so the teacher's job is never a straightforward business of inculcating specific skills. Education has become much more, and depends upon the 'special relationship' that the teacher has to establish with the child. This is the ground of the very particular Foucaultian notion of culture we are promoting.

In one of the schools studied there is a set of teaching guidelines available in the staff room, culled from a variety of sources. The advice for helping the backward reader is instructive, because it concentrates on many of the aspects of the teacher–child relationship discussed immediately above. The most important things are not the methods one should use, or the books that are best; what counts is the teacher's attitude – the ability to display a certain type of 'love':

Maintain the closest possible *personal contact* with the slow reader. Let him see from your attitude that you have a warm interest in him as a person, and that his happiness, welfare and progress are your constant concern. You will need to be consistent and not blow hot and cold in your relationships with him. (emphasis in original)

The teacher has been placed in a curious position; by virtue of access to social work files, s/he becomes part of a network of possible interventions into family life, yet s/he is also required to substitute almost directly for mothers (and fathers) who take no interest in the child's progress at school. As Ms Williamson relates:

There definitely are some, like, you know, like Jocelyn, for example. I mean, I think it's a matter of supreme indifference to her mother how she does at school. Then all her encouragement etcetera has to come from me.

Ms McCarthy then runs through the children on her register to tell the interviewer something about their reading. Every one is commented upon in terms of how their school work is supported by or obstructed by what happens at home. A typical example is her comment on Andrea:

Andrea's doing very well. She's a little hard-working girl. Nice parents who help her. And she's a nice child anyway, she is quite keen, you know, to learn.

The home is simultaneously the place that the teacher must somehow try to reconstruct in the school environment, with him/herself as a kind of substitute mother *and* the 'villain', to which failures in the education process are ultimately attributed. As Ms Williamson puts it, 'home predetermines everything'. No doubt, such a notion is credible mainly as a result of all those scientific enterprises which have shown both the importance of innate abilities in the child and the importance of the 'early years' in child development (for example, Central Advisory Council for Education 1967; Clarke and Clarke 1976). If the parents have let the child down by not providing enough stimulation in those years, then it makes the teacher's job almost impossible, so this thinking goes. In this way, it offers the teacher a kind of escape from what would otherwise be an overwhelming responsibility. Ms Williamson talks about Tracy, who is not quite a case for social welfare intervention, but the parents' lack of interest means there is nothing much she, as a teacher, can do:

Yeah, she's a pathetic little creature, she's in and out all the time. She's actually quite bright but because her attendance is so poor, she's never going to do much. She's sort of way . . . way down the list as far as progress in reading. It's a shame because she could do a lot better. Very little interest from home. You can tell to look at her, she looks pale and wan, uncared for.

When asked why Tracy's attendance is so poor, Ms Williamson replies,

Usually not very good reasons. Mother's waiting in for the electrician, they got up late, somebody was ill, somebody else was ill, this happened, that happened, you know, never especially good reasons, and often when she does come in her eyes are like that because she's been up late watching television. It's . . . it's not uncommon. . . . They'd know about any major problems, but I mean social work agencies are so understaffed and overworked that you can only deal with the really serious cases. Things like children going to bed after watching the midnight horror movie, I don't think they'll ever stop them, I mean, I've just known it throughout my teaching career.

The transformation of education into an interaction between the home and the school means that the teacher does not have to bear the ultimate responsibility for the 'failure' of the child. The teacher is finally confirmed as a mere facilitator of the process by the insertion of another piece into the theoretical jigsaw – the child as a natural learner:

> You know, you can also see children who are so . . . bright and hardworking etcetera, etcetera, and even a poor teacher isn't going to stop them . . . racing ahead.

Ms Williamson does more than confide her belief in these natural gifts in childhood to our interviewer, she also shows it at the teachers' self-help group she attends. Her notes from this group contain many statements which sketch out the exacting culture of teaching we are here describing: 'parents are crucial', 'children learn to read by reading', 'reading is a mixture of innate ability and environmental influence', 'teachers can help reading by providing motivation'. The process of reading is constructed along this typical nature/nurture axis and the delineation of the role of the parent and of the teacher is written into this grammar. Activity is a crucial way of eliciting these natural/environmental skills; reference in Ms Williamson's notes is made to Raban and Moon's (1978) work on reading as an 'active dialogue with the text'.

In such ways are the teachers' practices formed in relation to teaching reading; culture is very clearly a matter of (albeit very complex) management. Ideas about 'naturalness' or the importance of family life are inserted into the logic of the classroom almost at the level of common sense. From our Foucaultian perspective, of course, these practices and beliefs are far from natural; rather, they are the result of a very specific historical conjuncture and a set of important, although ultimately contingent, cultural transformations (Kendall 1991).

Teachers have access to a variety of academic psychological and educational literature which becomes part of their practice. One school has a (well-thumbed) copy of Henry Pearson's (1985) account of psycho-linguistics for teachers. The teachers in the staffroom spoke easily to the interviewer of their familiarity with psycho-linguistics as a theory of reading; they expressed knowledge of the work of Frank Smith, for example. In the teachers' reading education group, documents circulated include 'The Fallacy of Phonics' and 'Reading Readiness', which attempt to use Frank Smith's work to derogate these methods. For the teachers, meaningfulness should be the guide to everything: phonics is a bad idea because it does not put the stress on the overall meaning of the text; the concept of reading readiness is a bad one because, as Ms Williamson's notes put it, 'there is no moment in early schooling before which nothing concerned with reading could be achieved'.

Unsurprisingly, from our point of view, focusing as we are on culture as contingent management, an eclecticism informs most teachers' practice. So, elsewhere in Ms Williamson's notes is a section on the dangers of pushing children too hard. Ms Williamson has an insight into how her classroom practice has evolved:

> Um, I mean, it's a long time ago since I trained, twelve years ago, and it would perhaps be wrong for me to work from a theoretical basis in the first place if that theory came from college, because it's probably outdated anyway. Yes, and I learnt far more actually in the classroom than at college. That . . . teaching is about individual children and you can't learn about individuals in college, it's only when you're in the field, so to speak, that you learn to identify their particular needs, how they respond, how they are likely to respond, etcetera, etcetera.

It is clear that teachers do not simply buy into a set of theories, psychological or otherwise; teachers' practices are formed from a wider set of concerns. *They manage as best they can.* However, many of the theories that inform a teacher's practice become 'black-boxed', in the Latourian terminology we presented earlier; they become common sense and amalgamated into what appears to be a coherent practice. Attention to an individual's particular needs is one such 'common-sense' aspect of 'good teaching practice' that has become more and more prestigious in the classroom. Just as in the laboratory and in the factory, a body of scientific knowledge, which is never explicitly debated, allows for other practices to occur and to seem self-evident.

The teacher's instruction of the child in the classroom, then, is not simply a matter of the transmission of skills, but, through the formation of a 'special relationship' between the child and the teacher, it is also concerned with the production of a certain type of character. This is another arm of the Foucaultian approach to culture we are commending and reproducing here.

It is important to note that this education as more than just skill transmission is not an obligatory development, but is the result of an historically specific experiment. We can point to crucial figures in the construction of this 'extended' definition of education. David Stow, the noted education reformer, for example, convinced many to follow a series of experimental approaches to education which had emerged in continental Europe in the middle of the nineteenth century. Stow drew attention to the inefficient and, at times, 'negative' use of time and space in the classroom, and suggested that time and space be deployed more effectively as a technique for the production of good citizens. Stow was also a crucial figure in the institution of the playground as a site of moral training: the playground was theorised as a crucial space where children could 'let off steam', but also, under the watchful eye of the teacher, practise outside the lessons that had been learned inside. In a sense, the playground became the half-way house between the schoolroom and the community (Stow 1836, 1839, 1850; see also Tyler 1993). Stow's reforms of the school allowed a special relationship between the teacher and the pupil to be forged as a technique for citizen-production.

The teacher is advised 'gently to check, and mould, and lead . . . when firmly yet calmly checked, love and respect are engendered' (Stow 1850: 216). After Stow, the classroom became a space with a logic all its own, much more separate and distinct from the outside world than it had ever been before, but with its relationship to the outside world more clearly defined than hitherto. It is precisely in this respect that it became much more like a laboratory: an exclusive, experimental space where the results of specific strategies can be accurately assessed and new strategies accordingly invented and tried out. However, in becoming more and more like a laboratory, the classroom simultaneously became more like a factory, in that the desire to produce good, moral citizens became the guiding impulse. The classroom now had not only something like a recognisably modern moral tone, it also had a recognisably modern final aim: the manufacture of the young citizen.

The imperative for the teacher to 'love' the child, then, is connected to the reformulation of the classroom as an experimental but simultaneously productive space. As Schaffer (1992) has suggested, the beginning of the nineteenth century witnessed the invention of the modern 'scientific' self, a self whose conduct can be moulded and reformed by a whole series of scientific calculations. What Stow did was to graft on top of this new scientific self a vision of how the (child-)self should be cared for; the new 'pastoral technology', to borrow a phrase from Foucault (1981c), was one which, from its very beginnings, was legitimised by an appeal to the scientific and moral credentials of the production of the good future citizen.

Similarly, John Dewey was an important figure for the transformation in the classroom we are presenting. Early in our century, Dewey made a call for the classroom to be reconstituted as a 'learning environment'. As he puts it:

> The key to the present educational situation lies in the gradual reconstruction of school materials and methods so as to utilize various forms of occupation typifying social callings, and to bring out their intellectual and moral content. This reconstruction must relegate purely literary methods – including textbooks – and dialectical methods to the position of necessary auxiliary tools in cumulative activities. (Dewey 1915: 315)

The desire was to make this learning environment one which enabled the child to develop naturally, in accordance with his or her 'natural' interests.

This 'natural' development of the child is, of course, recognisable to us as the aim of modern liberal forms of education; yet this was no development for development's sake, but an attempt to fit out the individual for a role in society. Reading instruction needed to be made socially useful; the danger lay in conventional instruction, which 'may develop book worms, children who read omnivorously, but at the expense of development of social and executive abilities and skills' (Dewey 1929: 37). Dewey's fundamental concern here is a continuation of the transformation, perhaps first seen in Stow, of the classroom into a 'micro-community'. Education is a good thing, but it must be a specific form of education, that which manufactures a citizen able to take an active role in a participatory democracy.

With Stow and Dewey, we see clearly a vision of what the schoolroom might produce as a part of culture-as-management (or culture-as-government, or culture-as-administration) – what actors, what objects, and what ideas. To use the language we introduced earlier, this is a vision of the 'factory' aspects of schooling.

The end result of the schooling process thus became much more carefully defined and more and more of the apparently fundamental components of education (teachers, books, the transmission of skills) were downgraded until they were merely instrumental. It is unsurprising that Dewey's work opened up a path to recognisably Taylorist strategies in the management of American schools.

We see in Stow and Dewey, then, precursors of the logic of the modern classroom. The modern classroom continues their projects by educating in a way that installs culture, in the strict sense of the necessary skills for life, and in instrumentalising everything else. Reading is rarely taught as an abstract skill, but is brought within grander schemes, dreams and projects. The young reader can even be built as an entrepreneur, a particular example of schooling's role in culture-as-administration.

'Don't you think it's looking more like a question of complex management than dominant culture, Eric?' Meryl asked, genuinely seeking his views but also with an eye to checking his smugness level.

It must have been a high-smug day as Eric showed no sign of softening his hard line. 'If managing schooling to produce citizens isn't saturating kids with the dominant culture, what the hell is it?'

Eric was not asking a question and his aggressive tone, which had once enhanced their friendship, was now starting to annoy Meryl. 'Oh Eric, it's only like that if you're determined to see it like that. Why not leave the category of "citizen" open, rather than assuming it's some sort of bourgeois code for "member of the oppressed masses"?'

This was the first time Meryl had ever engaged in out-and-out argument with Eric. She liked it. He was shocked by her vehemence. He backed off a bit, but not much. 'Okay, think about it this way: the dominant culture produces schooling such that it produces the category "citizen" as if it were open.'

Meryl could tell that the slightly conciliatory tone did not signal a drop in Eric's smugness level; if anything, the reverse was true. She went further on the attack. 'Conspiracy thinking dressed in Althusserian clothes,' she boldly blurted, surprising herself at her boldness. It seemed to work – Eric went quiet. She took this rare occurrence as an acknowledgement from him, albeit a very grudging and subtle one, that there was something in her points. They tacitly agreed to a temporary cease-fire.

Training through choice   The classroom has become a training ground for young citizens, and reading is now firmly a technique used to attempt to produce in them the attributes of the full citizen. Reading instruction is oriented around the notion of choice, the *sine qua non* of participatory democracy. The child is never compelled to do anything, but is won over and in consequence buys into the benefits that literacy can bring. This is done through a variety of simple techniques. First of all, there is the library visit. When the child is at school, s/he can pick books freely from the school's own resources; however, the visit to the library is a much more explicit message to the child that the freedom to choose is part of learning to read. The child is invited slowly to learn an entrepreneurial attitude to the world of books; that is, the child can become something like an 'entrepreneur of the self', charged with the responsibility of choice and self-development.

The library visit, then, is never merely an instrument, a way of getting new books into the school; it is also a practice of freedom (Rose 1992a). The children rush around the library, some too excited to remember the rule about silence – they pick it up after a few visits – and select whatever they like. Often, of course, they select books that are inappropriate – much too hard or much too easy – and some have the curious habit of only picking out books they have already read. These children are gently coerced into making different selections, shown that they are in error and shown how they can stretch themselves.

On one particular visit to the library, a member of Ms Williamson's class, David, selects a pop-up book, much too easy for him considering how well his reading is going; Ms Williamson manages to convince him to put it back and get something else. She explains to the interviewer how she regards the book as too simple for David, and how his 'reason' for choosing the book is the wrong type of 'reason':

> Yeah, yeah, because he'd had that one, one of those that opened out into a big long [inaudible]. And that type of book I tend on the whole to discourage. . . . David was just getting that big long book for, for no good re- . . . because he liked the look of the book not . . . the actual . . .

The choice, then, is not simply about surface appeal, but comes to be tied to self-development. Unfortunately for Ms Williamson, another child manages to get the pop-up book out of the library, so when the interviewer talks to David about his book choice, he insists that he got the wrong book:

'What did you pick then David?'

'I picked. . . . I dunno. . . . That's the one, no, that's the one Miss Williamson gave to me.'

'Well, which one did you pick? Can you remember?'

'This one.' [points to pop-up book]

'Why do you like that one?'

'Cause it's got. . . . I'll show you. It does this.' [shows how book pops up]

David is still resistant to having his choice altered, but these are early days. Slowly the child's freedom to choose is transformed until such times as the child's 'free choice' is acceptable to the teacher. By the time our research project on these children was completed, some months later, such 'undesirable' choices were no longer being made.

'Choice', then, is slowly refined from something like a raw material, until it has become aligned with an external measure. As the child's book choice is tracked alongside a desired programme, so the child is simultaneously educated and made free (we should stress that for our Foucaultian approach to culture-as-administration this being 'made free' is treated seriously as a technique of liberal governance; for us, it is not a trick to hide some deeper agenda). In other areas, a similar tactic of manufacturing choice is employed and the children slowly learn to accept it. They are told to draw their own pictures and write their own stories, but the teacher walks around and suggests they do something else if their own choice is inappropriate. They are constituted as authors of these stories even though they are rewritten by the teacher if unacceptable.

In the two schools studied in our project, children were 'asked' what they wanted their 'stories' to be about. In these situations, they were usually 'fed' a topic sentence, such as 'I went to the shops on Saturday'. The teacher wrote out the sentence, and the children either wrote over the teacher's writing or copied underneath. They also drew a picture to accompany each story. On one notable occasion John wanted to write a story about going to prison to see his father. This was redrafted into something less delicate. Collette had a story about going to the electricity board with her mother to pay a bill, but the teacher redrafted it into something more aesthetically pleasing.

By such techniques are children produced as authors of their own – but officially sanctioned – accounts. Quickly enough, they learn to sanction their own accounts as they discover what is and is not appropriate in these exercises. In these ways, apparently minor school practices form an important part of culture-as-administration.

Surveillance as manufacture: examination   It will not be a surprise to anyone that the examination of children is considered an educational priority; witness this extract given out at an in-service training course, under the sub-heading 'The need for an objective test':

Teachers' opinions of children, no matter how expert, are liable to be highly subjective. What we want to know, regardless of other factors like running noses,
poor dress and speech, naughtiness, good arithmatic [*sic*] ability etc. (all of
which may cloud a teacher's judgement) is how does a child compare in reading
with average children of his age i.e. what is the average standard?

The teacher is given a procedure to obtain a score for the child, both in the
form of a reading age and in the form of a reading quotient. The teacher
has a simple and effective way of transforming the performance of the
child (in this instance, the ability to read words) into an 'objective' score.
S/he is thus furnished with the means to know and to make calculations
about the child in a scientific way. The in-service training course notes
include the following justifications for calculating a score for each child:

> We need to know a child's reading age so we can:
> 1. Put him [*sic*] on suitable reading matter.
> 2. Give him appropriate reading treatment. e.g. a 10 year old with a reading
>   age of 7.2 is an obvious candidate for remedial treatment; a 6 year old with
>   a reading age of 10 will require to be stretched well beyond the average level
>   of an infant class or acute boredom and under-achievement will result.
> 3. Put him in the right group.

For a Foucaultian understanding of culture, the most important thing to
note here is that the examination and the mark, the production of a new
sort of knowledge about the child through a specific means of 'capturing'
the child in an inscription, is not the operation of a negative power. The
examination is a technique of normalisation, but it is a normalising technique which has the amplification of capacities (cf. Rose 1992b) built into
it as a *raison d'être*. The child who is behind must be given remedial treatment; the child who is ahead must be stretched. These tests in fact form a
relatively minor part of the school timetable; they are regular but they are
not seen as the be-all-and-end-all of the school. As one school's 'Language
Policy' document states, 'Tests don't teach the child anything!'
    Other attempts to maximise the child's potential are given far more time
and attention than examination. One school, for example, runs a system
called 'Work Samples', a kind of dossier of the child's progress, but a
dossier where the child's work can speak for itself:

> The most important indicator of the work a child is doing is the child's own
> work. Consequently, the work samples are essential to enable the school to
> monitor progress in terms of rate and level of achievement. Whilst work samples
> are taken once each term, special pieces of work – both good and bad – may be
> relevant for inclusion in the files. In this way the files can become a true reflec-
> tion of the child's work.

These files are 'true reflections' precisely because they are a kind of democ-
ratisation of the process of evaluation. The child is the one producing the
work and the child, having taken on this prototypical authorial function,

can actually present his or her own work in the name of his or her own processes of development.

The test, then, is only one among many procedures schools have in their battery for developing the child. Another crucial technique, certainly in the schools studied by our project, is the additional language teaching given to children of ethnic minority parentage, under Section 11 of the 1966 British Local Government Act. Under the terms of this Act, Local Education Authorities may receive money for the employment of extra staff if they have to 'make special provision in the exercise of any of their functions in consequence of the presence within their areas of substantial numbers of immigrants from the Commonwealth whose language or customs differ from those of the rest of the community' (Home Office 1986).

Such interventions into the lives of children are, of course, easily criticised as manifestations of 'racist ideology', an attempt to substitute white bourgeois language and values for those of another ethnic group. But to approach these interventions in such a way is to miss an important point. The influence of 'race' has been inscribed in a particular way. In the schools studied, the child has to have both parents born in a foreign country (not just the Commonwealth) to be targeted for extra education. Once inscribed, 'race' is put into play in a series of calculations about the child. The potential dangers of something like Section 11 are obvious to the teachers and the schools; as one school handbook describes good practice, just after a piece on Section 11 and Remedial Education (which are, incidentally, strongly distinguished):

> This includes communication across the curriculum – the acquiring and passing on of knowledge, value [sic], beliefs and ideas. The children will learn as much from how we teach them as they do about what we teach them. We must ensure that opinions, beliefs and other value judgements are taught as such. We must avoid using methods or materials that may discriminate either openly or subconsciously and be able to justify everything we do.

All of this is to suggest that a Foucaultian analysis should not understand the sorts of practices put into play in the classroom as negative or as obstacles to complete development. The school is a factory–laboratory where children are manufactured out of educational experiments. The intention is not to deny children access to the truth about themselves, but to produce them as functioning, maximised citizens, to produce the truth about themselves. Culture actively works at producing citizens by management; it is not merely a repository of meanings.

Ms Williamson makes it quite clear that she understands the costs and gains of teaching children to read:

> I mean, to a certain extent, I suppose you're um . . . constantly urging the children to conform, but then in any institution you can only get by, in a sense, by, you know, by conforming. So I suppose that's a negative aspect to it. But on the

other hand, you're training them to take their part in society, so in that sense perhaps it's not negative, it's positive. I suppose it depends on where you're standing and how you're looking at it.

Techniques like those encouraged by Section 11 may well have a negative effect on children's consciousness of their own racial identity, but that is not the point of such measures. As Ms Williamson eloquently puts it, the point is 'training them to take their part in society'.

Summary: cultural studies as studies of meaning versus cultural studies as studies of management

Cultural studies as studies of meaning

- Use Foucault's methods like wall-filler products that promise certain results if you just 'aim and squirt', at whatever surface you care to pick.
- Use Foucault's methods to search the 'deep' water for 'deep' meaning, that is, use them as simply another resource in the study of culture as the site where hegemonic and resistant meanings ritually (and endlessly) do battle (for Hall, Foucault can thus help us confirm that '[n]o social practice exists outside of the domain of the semiotic – the practices and production of meaning').
- Use Foucault's methods but convert Foucault's understanding of power into only a synonym for membership of the board of the Culture Meaning-Bank – the powerful help stock the bank with those meanings which suit them, the powerless have no choice but to withdraw these meanings and eventually come to accept them as their own.
- Use Foucault's methods but forget that Foucault's books are specific histories of specific objects, not recipes for those interested in (half-) baking accounts of the meaning of modern life.

Cultural studies as studies of management

- Use Foucault's methods to produce accounts of particular cultural practices, such as schooling, which deliberately avoid reducing the complexity of historical change to simple stories of cause and effect and avoid exaggerating the importance of a set of local and contingent events by giving them an overarching logic or meaning.
- Use Foucault's methods to present culture as a set of governmental practices aimed at producing certain sorts of persons, not as a collection of phenomena which hold meanings like a bank, from which people withdraw and into which they deposit.
- Use Foucault's methods to help see cultural objects as ragbags of knowledge, practices and programmes gradually put together, with new practices being invented and old practices revitalised and pressed into service for new tasks.

- Use Foucault's methods to help understand culture in terms of the management of lives, not the meanings they drew on or left aside.
- Use Foucault's methods to help track forms of self, modes of ethical comportment, ways of knowing and of disciplining as products of particular cultural apparatuses, like the classroom, rather than pre-existing entities, thus helping to demonstrate that culture produces persons; it does not operate with and/or for pre-acculturated individuals. This 'culture' is not the site where individuals are imperfectly liberated, but rather the environment where persons are positively constructed within specific institutional forms, an arena which is productive of specific, historically localised forms of subjectivity, not a site for fostering a priori rational individuals, or a site for the repression and denial of true individuality.
- Use Foucault's methods to give a rather 'flat' description of the historical events involved in accounting for culture, because they deliberately eschew recourse to 'deeper' explanations of particular apparatuses or deeper meanings of the self. The cultural actor featured in this Foucaultian approach is thus not a bastardised or bowdlerised version of the 'true' self, a betrayal of what could have been and an obstacle to what should be – some artefact of 'genuine' culture.
- Use Foucault's methods to present the transmission of culture through schooling as a fragile practice, so contingent that it is hard to pick out an overarching logic or state-inspired programme, for example.
- Use Foucault's methods to help understand the classroom as a place for the constitution of young, autonomous citizens – an instance of the classroom as factory (there is an obvious 'product') and as laboratory (a series of experiments have been instituted to help this productive process).
- Use Foucault's methods to help show that ideas about 'naturalness' are inserted into the logic of the cultural institutions almost at the level of common sense. From our Foucaultian perspective, such 'naturalness' is always the result of a very specific historical conjuncture.
- Use Foucault's methods to help explore the ways the practitioners involved in the regular operation of cultural institutions *manage as best they can*, including the way different theories about how to proceed become 'black-boxed' – in Latourian terminology, the way they become common sense and amalgamated into what appears to be a coherent practice.
- Use Foucault's methods in a manner that allows us to see clearly a vision of what the schoolroom might produce as a part of culture-as-management (or culture-as-government, or culture-as-administration) – what actors, what objects, and what ideas.
- Use Foucault's methods to help build a picture of culture-as-administration in which being 'made free' and 'choosing' are treated seriously as techniques of liberal governance, rather than being seen as tricks to hide some deeper agenda.

- Use Foucault's methods to aid an understanding of the examination and the mark in terms of the production of a new sort of knowledge about the child through a specific means of 'capturing' the child in an inscription. This is not the operation of a negative power – the examination is a technique of normalisation, but it is a normalising technique which has the amplification of capacities built into it as a *raison d'être*.
- Use Foucault's methods in an account of culture that does not understand the sorts of practices put into play in the classroom as negative or as obstacles to complete development – the school is a factory – laboratory where children are manufactured out of educational experiments. The intention is not to deny children access to the truth about themselves, but to produce them as functioning, maximised citizens – to produce the truth about themselves; by this account, culture actively works at producing citizens by management.

It's your turn to try to use these points in the following exercise.

EXERCISE 5.3

Go through the various excerpts from the interviews with teachers and pupils included thus far and see if you can spot exactly where our analyses of them differ from the sort of analyses produced by the culture-as-meaning approach to cultural studies. Please consider at least three sets of pupils' and teachers' talk. Please write about 1,000 words in tackling this task.

A few more remarks

In establishing the advantages of an approach to culture which uses Foucault's methods to focus on management, or administration, rather than consciousness and meaning, we have concentrated on schooling as a part of culture (in the way we want you to see culture). We have dealt with some of the tactics of the modern classroom in relation to the teaching of reading, as a micro-example of culture at work. There are few spaces outside these practices where the child can refuse to be produced as a fulfilled citizen, armed with literacy and other techniques for living a particular sort of life. However, we do not want to suggest that there is no resistance. Perhaps it would be appropriate to include in this concluding section an anecdote about such forms of resistance.

Late in the school afternoon at one of the schools in our study the children have a playtime. When they come back after play they have a story. Then, for the last fifteen minutes of the school day, they finish off what they were doing before play. When they have finished their work they can 'choose', that is, select an activity such as a game to fill the rest of the time. One child, Michael, in the period leading up to play, worked laboriously slowly on his story day after day. In fact, it was clear that he had finished his story but spun out time with some extra colouring in, tracing over of letters, and so on. He finished his work each day exactly at the moment when the teacher said it was time for play. One day, the interviewer went over to him and asked why, given that he had obviously finished his story, he didn't show it to the teacher. He replied that he couldn't do that, for if he did, the teacher would make him start something else and he would have to finish it off when he returned from play. Michael was keen to be able to 'choose' after play. At five years of age, after a term at school, Michael had begun to work out how institutions operate.

In the modern primary school classroom one can see culture as the sometimes uneasy co-existence of a variety of practices connected to a variety of forms of life. Many of these forms can be made visible by attending to the problem of literacy in the classroom. We have characterised the classroom as a learning environment which suits the demands of the modern liberal state: children are produced as young citizens, authors of their own works, free and independent, able to choose the path of their learning, but within the confines of liberal governance.

The 'uneasy co-existence' we mentioned above has to do, at least in part, with resistance to the 'amplification of capacities'. Children in the modern classroom may well be able to devise complex strategies of resistance, as do their teachers. However, out of this confusing and confused set of activities arises a regular, daily pedagogical practice which facilitates the production of the literate citizen. Mundane culture-as-administration, rather than the more familiar yet more dramatic culture-as-meaning-bank, is the canvas on which the school as part-laboratory, part-factory is best painted.

Eric was feeling decidedly poorly. By this stage he knew in his heart that Meryl's doubts about their original culture-as-meaning enthusiasm were well founded, that to approach culture as a diverse set of administrative operations is a much better use of Foucault's methods in regard to cultural studies. However, Eric's heart could say nothing to his head. His head decided to go down swinging.

'I'm far from convinced,' he said, barely convincing himself. 'If we're going to use the factory metaphor, let's use it accurately: schools are like factories because they train kids to work in factories, not because they produce anything.'

Meryl knew now, with the certainty that Eric lacked, that their original position had been wrong-headed. She felt like simply ignoring Eric's outburst, but the bond of their friendship still had some glue. 'Be serious Eric, you know as well as I do that you're only using half the metaphor. Have you forgotten that we came into the cultural studies business armed with both Foucault and Latour; the school is a combination of factory and laboratory – the production of citizens is not factory-like in that old-leftie, mass-production sense, but in the sense of flexible, can't-be-certain-of-the-outcome sense.'

Eric could only grumble that it sounded a bit romantic to him, but he didn't have the argumentative energy left to make anything of it.

Part III

CONCLUSION

6

'Is Foucault a party animal?'

CONTENTS

We're in a very fortunate position to tackle the question in this chapter's title as we were able to assume fly-on-the-wall status at a recent student party at which Foucault was much discussed, if not always appreciated. Here's our report.

'Looks like a good party Dermie', Devon said tentatively, as they approached the front door.

'I must be out of my mind, letting you talk me into something like this. You know I loathe the sort of characters likely to be here. Don't be surprised if you see me making a break for the comfort of my remote control.' This was the most Dermot had said to Devon for months, so even though it was far from cheerful, Devon took it as a sign of a growing friendship between them.

Barely had they found a drink when they had to deal with a loudmouth whose name they couldn't quite catch. Dermot didn't really want to catch it: he thought it was Enzo; Devon heard Inzy. Of course it was Inzammam, and he was little different than when we met him in Chapter 1. He'd only had two beers, but that was enough for him to think everyone he bumped into must be keen to hear his latest thinking.

'You two look like scholarly types. I think I've convinced just about everyone here that sex nowadays is much less repressed than this time last century,' he babbled, no nearer to a realisation that Foucault's histories never stop than the last time we saw him.

Devon felt compelled to argue with him. Dermot felt compelled to head for his small screen. As he was ducking out he couldn't avoid saying hello to a woman he knew vaguely from the last party he'd endured. It was Jenny.

'Are you running away too?' she asked, almost rhetorically.

'Is it that obvious?' Dermot felt relieved that Jenny instantly identified herself as a fellow sufferer.

'I don't mind chatting about intellectual things at a party – at least not after a few drinks, which I've now had – but that Inzammam just pushes it too far,' she said.

Dermot felt even more relief. 'Don't worry,' he said with his customary mock seriousness, 'now that he's got Devon's ear, you'll be safe for hours.'

Jenny offered him some of her wine and his desire to flee abated, for a while anyway. They chatted easily enough, Jenny confessing as they did, after more wine, that she still felt very uncertain about 'all this Foucault business'. Dermot was in the process of reassuring her by telling her that he didn't think anyone had a complete grasp of it when they heard a mix of laughter and loud talking about the very man coming from the next room. They inched in.

Steffi found enough 'Dutch courage' to make a suggestion about how the proposed quiz should work. 'No. Instead, why don't we each write down some things that sound like "Foucault things", put them in a hat or something, then when each contestant draws one out, he or she has to say whether it really is a Foucaultian point and what it's about?'

Eric, always quick to take over other people's suggestions, grabbed back the organising role. 'Nice one. Let's make it that we write down four things each to begin with – one on archaeology, one on genealogy, one on discourse and one on power–knowledge – and let's make it a mix of sensible and silly or it won't work.'

Dermot instantly thought Eric a complete prat, but for once he held his tongue, for Jenny's sake. He noticed she was beaming at the idea of the quiz, and even though this meant she slipped a notch or two on his 'Dermograph', he decided to just grin and bear it. He joined in the game, but only half-heartedly. He seemed to be the only one irritated by Eric's manner as he organised everyone's 'hat' entries.

'Righto everyone!' Eric shouted, 'here we go. First contestant please.'

Zeeha is the volunteering type in these situations and she grabbed the room's attention with her insistent 'Pick me, pick me!'

'Well, young lady,' Eric said, doing another of his sad impressions, this time of a quiz show host, 'tell us this, if you will: are any of the following items descriptions of research tools developed by the great Michel Foucault, and if so, which ones: one, "a tool which describes statements in the archive, statements covering the said, the unsaid and the visible"; two "a tool which analyses the relation between one's state of mind and the state of the pitch" [some giggling as he read this one out, though only squirming from Dermot]; three, a tool which "introduces power through a history of the present, concerned with disreputable origins and unpalatable functions"; and four, "a tool which demands the identification of rules that delimit the sayable (which of course are never rules of closure)".'

Zeeha jumped in quickly. 'One is serious and about archaeology. Two is boys' nonsense. Three is easy – genealogy. And four is Foucault's way of using power and knowledge together to help free the oppressed.'

Everyone (except Dermot) cheered and laughed, mostly at her machine-gun delivery.

'Right on, sister,' Eric announced, 'but not quite right. I'd like to tell you that *number two is only "boys' nonsense" for those who don't understand working-class culture, but in this company I'd better not [more laughter, again without Dermot's support]. Seriously though, number four is about discourse. Next please.'*

'I'll have a go at it!' enthused Curtly. 'Sexuality here, there, then and now, that's my motto.' Encouraging hoots sprang from the audience. Something else sprang from Dermot's stomach, but he managed to keep it in.

Eric straightaway warmed to his new interlocutor. 'Yeah baby, let's dig the culture here, there, then and now.'

The two of them fell about laughing. Most everyone else present at least had a chuckle. Dermot nearly fainted with incredulity at this twosome of terror. How could they get it so wrong, he wondered, still to himself, now convinced that escape was his only salvation. He made a dash for his truly beloved – the TV – yet again. Yet again he didn't make it. He was waylaid this time by the siren call of mocking laughter – something which always attracts him.

'Why don't we try it while gargling the Latour red?' asked Martina of Iva, in a tone that let Dermot know they were mocking the game going on in the next room.

Sensing the company of his sort of people, he tried his hand. 'While balancing ten copies of We Have Never Been Modern *on your nose?' he chipped in as a suggestion.*

The girls quickly recognised a soul-mate in distress. 'Only if it's the new edition, re-titled We Have Never Been Sensible,*' Iva shot back.*

Faster than the speed of a black box slamming shut, the three of them had their own mock quiz going in the corner, about science, modernity and other scallops – sustained by the red they continued to insist to one another was straight from Bruno's family vineyard. To their ears wit crackled between them, though to our fly-on-the-wall senses it was more wine than wit.

'Does "scientific essentialism" include the idea that science is something special and distinct from other forms of cultural and social activity, or the idea that "great men" discover "real-world" objects in the manner that Callon discovered scallops?' Iva teased.

Dermot was sharp. 'Latour turned sociology of knowledge on its head, like fomenting champagne, seeing science producing truth and telling us all about it, so the answer to your question has to be the "great man" thesis.'

'Very clever my caped scholar,' Martina mimicked, the three of them by now convinced they were performing a merciless parody of events in the next room with the panache of a Gielgud, 'but riddle me this: given that black boxing helps scientists go about their work by simplifying the complexities of the social world, is said black boxing a device to break down the distinction between macro- and micro-actors, or a world heavyweight contest?'

As there's no stopping this sort of run-away humour-in-its-own-land, we'll cut to the moment when, suitably fortified, Iva, Martina and Dermot decided to disrupt Eric's quiz, which by this time had become Eric and Curtly's quiz.

EXERCISE 6.1

You may as well have an opportunity to join in the three mockske-teers' game. We'll give you a list of some random points from our various discussions of science, scallops and the like and you can build your own mock quiz. We think they lend themselves to the task. Please try to incorporate at least three of the following points:

- Latour's notion of 'black boxing' involves leaving elements out of consideration (for example, in driving a car we know about only some elements of the car – the black box is what we rely on but do not examine).
- In keeping the lids on so many black boxes, science employs two main tactics – displacing goals and inventing new goals.
- A big advantage of the Latourian use of Foucault's methods is that it avoids technological determinism. Accounts of the changes wrought by the development of the stirrup or of certain weapons are instances of this type of determinism.
- The translations that take place in socio-technical systems invent a geography of obligatory points of passage. New developments must work through those which have come to dominate (for example, the development of any new fridge technologies must now work through the electric fridge).
- Modernism has a misleading approach to temporality.
- Related to this, modernism makes a false distinction between the contingent and the necessary.
- On a similar theme, modernism can only conceptualise history as revolutions.
- Postmodernism refuses the task of empirical description as 'sci-entistic' (modernist), yet it accepts the modernist idea of dividing time into successive revolutions, leaving it in the 'ludicrous' posi-tion of coming after the moderns while arguing against the idea of any 'after'.
- Postmodernism is 'simply stuck in the impasse of all avant-gardes that have no more troops behind them'.
- Postmodernism is a symptom, not a solution.
- In the scallops and fishermen story, the researchers attempted to make the network (of knowledge and actors) as strong as possible by the process of *interessement*, the act of attempting to stabilise the identity of another actant by stabilising its own links with that entity and weakening the links the entity has with other entities.
- *Interessement* does not always work; actants do not always accept the roles that are constructed for them. In this example, the enrol-ments involved were not accepted. The scallops refused to anchor,

and some fishermen could not resist fishing the stocks the researchers built up. The scallops' abilities to anchor were now cast into doubt; the fishermen's desire to see the long-term restocking of the Bay was likewise now a dubious proposition. In this case, social and natural phenomena were reorganised in the same way.

- Latour's account of the development of the automatic door-closer – the way feelings and desires are, literally, incorporated into this nonhuman delegate such that it incorporates the injunction to keep the door closed and still incorporates the possibility to get more complex, such that it might open doors as you approach, ask you to prove your identity, shut in dangerous situations, etc. – shows us the ways in which the distinction between human and nonhuman, the sacred boundary of the social sciences, is less interesting than the gradient of delegation, which ranges from the complete moral human being to the efficient machine.
- In refusing to differentiate between humans and nonhumans or between nature and society a priori, Latour and Callon's examples suggest a completely new form of sociology which reintegrates nature and nonhumans into knowledge and networks. They ask us to see how interpretations emerge from networks, rather than assuming that we know in advance how networks are structured, assuming that we know how society works.

Eric and Curtly were ruthlessly quizzing a steely eyed Meryl as Iva, Martina and Dermot returned to the fray. The two know-it-all quiz-masters seemed oblivious to Meryl's grim determination that they were not going to embarrass her and our three intrepid quiz-busters spontaneously decided to rescue her.

Eric and Curtly were revelling in each other's company as they pushed the game into the cultural studies region they felt to be their home ground. Iva, Martina and Dermot took them on by answering their silly questions seriously. Here are just some of the exchanges that marked the battle.

'Which of these four is pure Michel: one, Foucault's methods can yield good political analysis when applied to all sites of working-class culture; two, Foucault's methods help find the deeper meanings of culture under the surface of capitalist consumption; three, Foucault's methods allow an understanding of the power of the bourgeoisie to impose Victorian sexual morality; and four, Foucault's methods are recipes for those interested in the full story of the meaning of modern life,' Eric beamed.

Curtly belted out an answer before Meryl could open her mouth. 'All of them are spot on because I wrote them!'

Eric, laughing with Curtly, now almost in a world of two with him, started into one of his ridiculous 'high fives' when Dermot cut him short with a booming voice that surprised everyone present, including Dermot himself. 'If you two clowns are going to ask questions, you should at least let the contestant answer them properly.'

'We've answered them properly for her,' Eric retorted, only marginally put off his stride by Dermot's intervention.

He was pushed a little further off it by another surprisingly loud and quick interjection, this time from Martina. 'Number one is pure twaddle not pure Michel. Foucault's methods should be used to produce accounts of particular cultural practices, such as schooling, accounts which avoid simple stories of cause and effect and avoid giving these practices any overarching meaning.'

Curtly stepped in to prop up the tottering Eric, though he was none too sure of himself (we knew what he'd been through in Chapter 2, but hardly anyone else there did). 'Oh, come on, surely you've got to allow for some deeper meaning?'

His timid support wasn't much help. It seemed only to inspire Meryl, who found her voice and took up the lead Dermot and Martina had offered. 'Rather than power, bourgeoisie and capitalist classes, you should be using Foucault's methods to explore the ways culture operates as a set of governmental practices aimed at producing certain sorts of persons.'

Curtly wilted quickly, the experience of having the rug pulled from under him in the classroom suddenly rushing back to him. Eric, as we would expect, wasn't prepared to give it up so easily. He could sense the rest of the people in the room siding with the foursome of Meryl and the three blow-ins. Perhaps he mistook a mood of 'party-goers vicariously enjoying any argument' as support for his opponents, but whatever, he could feel the corner racing at him and you know what he's like when trapped in a corner. 'You people know nothing about modern life and nothing about Foucault. You haven't got the brains of a sheep.'

Iva was the one who took the broom to him in his corner. 'Foucault's methods are useful to explore the management of lives, you moron, not their meanings. His methods are flat, like your head. If we haven't got the brains of a sheep, you certainly have.'

The room erupted into quiz-ending laughter. Sentence fragments from the four victors hung in the air, jocularly repeated by some – 'cultural objects as ragbags of knowledge, practices and programmes gradually put together', 'forms of self, modes of ethical comportment, ways of knowing and of disciplining as products of particular cultural apparatuses', 'the Foucaultian approach isn't a bastardised or bowdlerised version of the "true" self, a betrayal of what could have been and an obstacle to what should be', 'being "made free" and "choosing" should be treated seriously as techniques of liberal governance, rather than being seen as tricks to hide some deeper agenda'.

Our four heroes decided to leave together, feeling pretty good about themselves as they did. A buoyant mood was a rare treat for Dermot. Even the sight of Devon still arguing in drunken circles with Inzammam wasn't enough to dampen his spirits. In fact he teased Dev with a cryptic, 'I am looking for a man. Do you have a lamp?' as he went by.

Devon thought Dermot had lost it, but Dermot knew otherwise.

Guide to further reading

While our students have been struggling with Foucault's methods, at least some of them have also been doing their reading. Here are some suggestions from their lists:

Foucault on his methods

Foucault, M. (1981a) 'Questions of Method'. *I&C* 8, 3–14. This is reprinted in Burchell, G., Gordon, C. and Miller, P. (eds) *The Foucault Effect: Studies in Governmentality.* Hemel Hempstead: Harvester Wheatsheaf, 1991.
Foucault, M. (1981b) 'The Order of Discourse'. In Young, R. (ed.) *Untying the Text: A Post-Structuralist Reader.* London: Routledge and Kegan Paul.
Florence, M. (1998) 'Foucault'. In Foucault, M. *Aesthetics, Method, and Epistemology: Essential Works of Foucault, 1954–1984.* New York: New Press.
Foucault, M. (1972) *The Archaeology of Knowledge.* London: Tavistock, especially Introduction (pp. 3–17), Part I Chapter 1 (pp. 21–30), and Part IV Chapter 1 (pp. 135–140).
Foucault, M. (1977) 'Nietzsche, Genealogy, History'. In Bouchard, D.F. (ed.) *Michel Foucault. Language, Counter-Memory, Practice: Selected Essays and Interviews.* Ithaca: Cornell University Press. This is reprinted in Rabinow, P. (ed.) *The Foucault Reader.* Harmondsworth: Penguin, 1984.
Foucault, M. (1991) 'Politics and the Study of Discourse'. In Burchell, G., Gordon, C. and Miller, P. (eds) *The Foucault Effect: Studies in Governmentality.* Hemel Hempstead: Harvester Wheatsheaf.
Foucault, M. (1998) 'On the Ways of Writing History'. In *Aesthetics, Method, and Epistemology: Essential Works of Foucault, 1954–1984.* New York: New Press.
Foucault, M. (1998) 'On the Archaeology of the Sciences: Response to the Epistemology Circle'. In *Aesthetics, Method, and Epistemology: Essential Works of Foucault, 1954–1984.* New York: New Press.

We suggest you read these pieces in the order we have set out above.

Other writers on Foucault's methods

Dean, M. (1994) *Critical and Effective Histories: Foucault's Methods and Historical Sociology.* London: Routledge, especially Chapters 1 and 2. This book is an indispensable guide to Foucault's idiosyncratic view of history, and situates Foucault's work among other approaches to history.
Deleuze, G. (1986) *Foucault.* London: Athlone. This book is hard-going, but it presents a view of Foucault by a great philosopher in his own right, a man who was very

close to Foucault. You might notice that Deleuze traces Foucault's methodological innovations to his philosophical considerations – even the emphasis on power is understood in this way, rather than as a response to political problems.

Veyne, P. (1997) 'Foucault Revolutionizes History'. In Davidson, A. (ed.) *Foucault and his Interlocutors*. Chicago: University of Chicago Press. Paul Veyne is another writer who was very close to Foucault. This piece deals carefully with the notion of 'rarity' in Foucault's method. It also expands on the materiality of discourse that we discussed in relation to Ian Hunter in Chapter 2 and to John Law in Chapter 3.

Macey, D. (1993) *The Lives of Michel Foucault*. London: Random House. This is one of the biographies of Foucault (there were three at the last count). It includes many useful points about methodology.

More general guides to method

Silverman, D. (1993) *Interpreting Qualitative Data: Methods for Analysing Talk, Text and Interaction*. London: Sage.

Silverman, D. (ed.) (1997) *Qualitative Research: Theory, Method and Practice*. London: Sage (particularly the chapter by Lindsay Prior – 'Following in Foucault's Footsteps: Texts and Context in Qualitative Research').

These texts deal with a variety of approaches besides the Foucaultian, but are very useful in helping you to think through specific methods you will need for specific research problems.

Uses of Foucault

As you will no doubt be aware, there are many books and articles claiming to be inspired by Foucault. The following are perhaps the most instructive:

Hacking, I. (1991) 'How Should We Do the History of Statistics?' In Burchell, G., Gordon, C. and Miller, P. (eds) *The Foucault Effect: Studies in Governmentality*. Hemel Hempstead: Harvester Wheatsheaf. This provides a close reading of Foucault's methods and then shows the reader, in quick time, how they can be used to analyse Hacking's own area of interest.

Rose, N. (1985) *The Psychological Complex: Psychology, Politics and Society in England 1869–1939*. London: Routledge and Kegan Paul. The methodology of this book is not really foregrounded. However, it is an excellent example of how Foucault's methods can be put to use to transform accepted histories (in this case, of the psychology of individual differences and of psychology more generally).

On methods for studying science

Latour, B. (1992) 'Where are the Missing Masses?' In Bijker, W. and Law, J. (eds) *Shaping Technology/Building Society*. Cambridge, Mass.: MIT Press.

Latour, B. (1986) 'The Powers of Association'. In Law, J. (ed.) *Power, Action and Belief*. London: Routledge and Kegan Paul.

Latour, B. (1991) 'Technology is Society Made Durable'. In Law, J. (ed.) *A Sociology of Monsters*. London: Routledge.

Callon, M. (1986b) 'Some Elements of a Sociology of Translation: Domestication of the

Scallops and the Fishermen of St Brieuc Bay'. In Law, J. (ed.) *Power, Action, and Belief*. London: Routledge and Kegan Paul.

Callon, M. (1986a) 'The Sociology of an Actor-Network: The Case of the Electric Vehicle'. In Callon, M., Law, J. and Rip, A. (eds) *Mapping the Dynamics of Science and Technology*. London: Macmillan.

Law, J. (1994) *Organizing Modernity*. Oxford: Blackwell, especially pp. 1–30.

These pieces may only be familiar to you from our discussions in Chapters 3 and 4. If so, we suggest you read them in the order we have set out above.

References

Althusser, L. (1971) 'Ideology and Ideological State Apparatuses (Notes towards an Investigation)'. In *Lenin and Philosophy and Other Essays*. New York: Monthly Review Press.

Annas, J. and Barnes, J. (1994) 'Introduction'. In Sextus Empiricus *Outlines of Scepticism*. Cambridge: Cambridge University Press.

Bachelard, G. (1968) *The Philosophy of No: A Philosophy of the New Scientific Mind*. New York: Viking.

Bachelard, G. (1986) *The New Scientific Spirit*. New York: Farrar, Straus & Giroux.

Benchley, R. (1937) 'Shakespeare Explained: Carrying on the System of Footnotes to a Silly Extreme'. In Laycock, S. (ed.) *The Greatest Pages of American Humour: A Study of the Rise and Development of Humorous Writings in America with Selections from the Most Notable of the Humorists*. London: Methuen.

Bennington, G. (1988) *Lyotard: Writing the Event*. Manchester: Manchester University Press.

Bevis, P., Cohen, M. and Kendall, G. (1993) 'Archaeologizing Genealogy: Michel Foucault and the Economy of Austerity'. In Gane, M. and Johnson, T. (eds) *Foucault's New Domains*. London: Routledge.

Boltanski, L. and Thévenot, L. (1987) *Les Économies de la grandeur, cahiers du Centre d'Études de l'Emploi 31*. Paris: Presses Universitaires de France.

Bowles, S. and Gintis, H. (1976) *Schooling in Capitalist America: Educational Reform and the Contradictions of Economic Life*. New York: Basic Books.

Brannigan, A. (1981) *Social Bases of Scientific Discovery*. Cambridge: Cambridge University Press.

Brunt, R. (1989) 'The Politics of Identity'. In Hall, S. and Jacques, M. (eds) *New Times: The Changing Face of Politics in the 1990s*. London: Lawrence and Wishart.

Butterfield, J. (1996) 'Studies in Pyrrhonism'. Unpublished MS, Murdoch University, Perth.

Callon, M. (1986a) 'The Sociology of an Actor-Network: The Case of the Electric Vehicle'. In Callon, M., Law, J. and Rip, A. (eds) *Mapping the Dynamics of Science and Technology*. London: Macmillan.

Callon, M. (1986b) 'Some Elements of a Sociology of Translation: Domestication of the Scallops and the Fishermen of St Brieuc Bay'. In Law, J. (ed.) *Power, Action, and Belief*. London: Routledge and Kegan Paul.

Callon, M. and Latour, B. (1981) 'Unscrewing the Big Leviathan: How Actors Macro-Structure Reality and How Sociologists Help Them to Do So'. In Knorr-Cetina, K. and Cicourel, A. (eds) *Advances in Social Theory and Methodology*. London: Routledge and Kegan Paul.

Callon, M. and Latour, B. (1992) 'Don't Throw the Baby out with the Bath School! A Reply to Collins and Yearley'. In Pickering, A. (ed.) *Science as Practice and Culture*. Chicago: University of Chicago Press.

Canguilhem, G. (1989) *The Normal and the Pathological*. New York: Zone Books.

Canguilhem, G. (1990) *Ideology and Rationality in the History of the Life Sciences*. Cambridge, Mass.: MIT Press.

Canguilhem, G. (1994) *A Vital Rationalist: Selected Writings from Georges Canguilhem*. New York: Zone Books.

Central Advisory Council for Education (1967) *Children and their Primary Schools (The Plowden Report)*. London: HMSO.

Chandler, A. (1977) *The Visible Hand: The Managerial Revolution in American Business*. Cambridge, Mass.: Harvard University Press.

Chomsky, N. (1965) *Aspects of the Theory of Syntax*. Cambridge, Mass.: MIT Press.

Clarke, A.M. and Clarke, A.D.B. (1976) *Early Experience: Myth and Evidence*. Oxford: Open Books.

Collins, H.M. (1985) *Changing Order*. London: Sage.

Collins, H.M. (1987) 'Certainty and Public Understanding of Science: Science on Television'. *Social Studies of Science* 17, 689–713.

Collins, H.M. (1988) 'Public Experiments and Displays of Virtuosity: The Core-Set Revisited'. *Social Studies of Science* 18, 725–48.

Collins, H.M. and Pinch, T.J. (1979) 'The Construction of the Paranormal'. In Wallis, R. (ed.) *On the Margins of Science*. Keele: University of Keele Press.

Collins, H.M. and Yearley, S. (1992) 'Epistemological Chicken'. In Pickering, A. (ed.) *Science as Practice and Culture*. Chicago: University of Chicago Press.

Corrigan, P. and Sayer, D. (1985) *The Great Arch: State Formation as Cultural Revolution*. Oxford: Blackwell.

Cowan, R. (1985) 'How the Refrigerator Got its Hum'. In Mackenzie, D. and Wajcman, J. (eds) *The Social Shaping of Technology*. Milton Keynes: Open University Press.

Dean, M. (1994) *Critical and Effective Histories: Foucault's Methods and Historical Sociology*. London: Routledge.

Deleuze, G. (1986) *Foucault*. London: Athlone.

Deleuze, G. and Guattari, F. (1988) 'Rhizome'. In *A Thousand Plateaus: Capitalism and Schizophrenia*. London: Athlone.

Dewey, J. (1915) *Democracy and Education*. New York: Free Press.

Dewey, J. (1929) *The Sources of a Science of Education*. New York: Horace Liveright.

Donald, J. (1992) *Sentimental Education: Schooling, Popular Culture and the Regulation of Liberty*. London: Verso.

During, S. (1992) *Foucault and Literature: Towards a Genealogy of Writing*. London: Routledge.

Durkheim, É. (1915) *The Elementary Forms of the Religious Life*. London: Allen and Unwin.

Fayard, P. (1993) 'Daily Science in the European Quality Press'. In Durant, J.A. and Gregory, J. (eds) *Science and Culture in Europe*. London: Science Museum.

Feyerabend, P. (1975) *Against Method*. London: New Left Books.

Foucault, M. (1970) *The Order of Things: An Archaeology of the Human Sciences*. London: Tavistock.

Foucault, M. (1972) *The Archaeology of Knowledge*. London: Tavistock.

Foucault, M. (1973) *The Birth of the Clinic: An Archaeology of Medical Perception*. New York: Pantheon.

Foucault, M. (1977) *Discipline and Punish: The Birth of the Prison*. London: Allen Lane.

Foucault, M. (1978a) 'Conférence inédite à la Societé Française de Philosophie', May. Typescript at Bibliothèque le Saulchoir, Paris.

Foucault, M. (1978b) *The History of Sexuality Volume I: An Introduction*. New York: Pantheon.

Foucault, M. (1980a) 'Prison Talk'. *Radical Philosophy* 16, 10–15. In Gordon, C. (ed.) *Michel Foucault. Power/Knowledge: Selected Interviews and Other Writings 1972–1977*. Brighton: Harvester.

Foucault, M. (1980b) 'Two Lectures'. In Gordon, C. (ed.) *Michel Foucault. Power/Knowledge: Selected Interviews and Other Writings 1972–1977*. Brighton: Harvester.

Foucault, M. (1980c) 'Truth and Power'. In Gordon, C. (ed.) *Michel Foucault. Power/Knowledge: Selected Interviews and Other Writings 1972–1977*. Brighton: Harvester.

Foucault, M. (1981a) 'Questions of Method'. *I&C* 8, 3–14.

Foucault, M. (1981b) 'The Order of Discourse'. In Young, R. (ed.) *Untying the Text: A Post-Structuralist Reader*. London: Routledge and Kegan Paul.

Foucault, M. (1981c) ' "Omnes et Singulatim": Towards a Criticism of Political Reason'. In McMurrin, S.M. (ed.) *The Tanner Lectures on Human Values*. Cambridge: Cambridge University Press.

Foucault, M. (1982) 'The Subject and Power'. An Afterword to Dreyfus, H. and Rabinow, P. *Michel Foucault: Beyond Structuralism and Hermeneutics*. Chicago: University of Chicago Press.

Foucault, M. (1984) 'What is Enlightenment?' In Rabinow, P. (ed.) *The Foucault Reader*. New York: Pantheon.

Foucault, M. (1986) *The Care of the Self: The History of Sexuality Volume III*. New York: Pantheon.

Foucault, M (1988a) 'The Art of Telling the Truth'. In Kritzman, L.D. (ed.) *Michel Foucault. Politics, Philosophy, Culture: Interviews and Other Writings of Michel Foucault, 1977–1984*. New York: Routledge.

Foucault, M (1988b) 'The Masked Philosopher'. In Kritzman, L.D. (ed.) *Michel Foucault. Politics, Philosophy, Culture: Interviews and Other Writings of Michel Foucault, 1977–1984*. New York: Routledge.

Foucault, M (1988c) 'Practising Criticism'. In Kritzman, L.D. (ed.) *Michel Foucault. Politics, Philosophy, Culture: Interviews and Other Writings of Michel Foucault, 1977–1984*. New York: Routledge.

Foucault, M. (1991) *Remarks on Marx: Conversations with Duccio Trombadori*. New York: Semiotext(e).

Gooding, D. (1985) 'In Nature's School: Faraday as an Experimentalist'. In Gooding, D. and James, F.A. (eds) *Faraday Rediscovered: Essays on the Life and Work of Michael Faraday, 1791–1876*. London: Macmillan.

Gutmann, A. (1987) *Democratic Education*. Princeton: Princeton University Press.

Hacking, I. (1975) *The Emergence of Probability*. Cambridge: Cambridge University Press.

Hacking, I. (1990) *The Taming of Chance*. Cambridge: Cambridge University Press.

Hacking, I. (1992a) 'Multiple Personality Disorder and its Hosts'. *History of the Human Sciences* 5(2), 3–31.

Hacking, I. (1992b) 'The Self-Vindication of the Laboratory Sciences'. In Pickering, A. (ed.) *Science as Practice and Culture*. Chicago: University of Chicago Press.

Hall, S. (1980) 'Cultural Studies: Two Paradigms'. *Media, Culture and Society* 2, 57–72.

Hall, S. (1988a) *The Hard Road to Renewal: Thatcherism and the Crisis of the Left*. London: Verso.

Hall, S. (1988b) 'The Toad in the Garden: Thatcherism among the Theorists'. In Nelson, C. and Grossberg, L. (eds) *Marxism and the Interpretation of Culture*. Champagne-Urbana: University of Illinois Press.

Hall, S. (1988c) 'Brave New World'. *Marxism Today*, October, 24–9.

Hankinson, R.J. (1995) *The Sceptics*. London: Routledge.

Henriques, J., Hollway, W., Urwin, C., Venn, C. and Walkerdine, V. (1984) *Changing the Subject: Psychology, Social Regulation and Subjectivity*. London: Methuen.

Home Office (1986) *Circular 72/1986*. London: HMSO.

Hoskin, K. (1993) 'Education and the Genesis of Disciplinarity: The Unexpected Reversal'. In Messer-Davidow, E., Shumway, D.R. and Sylvan, D.J. (eds)

Knowledges: Historical and Critical Studies in Disciplinarity. Charlottesville: University of Virginia Press.

Hoskin, K. and Macve, R.H. (1993) 'Accounting as Discipline: The Overlooked Supplement'. In Messer-Davidow, E., Shumway, D.R. and Sylvan, D.J. (eds) *Knowledges: Historical and Critical Studies in Disciplinarity*. Charlottesville: University of Virginia Press.

Hunt, A. and Wickham, G. (1994) *Foucault and Law: Towards a Sociology of Law as Governance*. London: Pluto.

Hunter, I. (n.d.) 'Michel Foucault: Discourse versus Language'. Unpublished MS, Griffith University, Brisbane.

Hunter, I. (1989) *Culture and Government: The Emergence of Literary Education*. Basingstoke: Macmillan.

Hunter, I. (1994) *Rethinking the School: Subjectivity, Bureaucracy, Criticism*. Sydney: Allen and Unwin.

Jenkins, R. (1975) 'Technology and the Market: George Eastman and the Origins of Mass Amateur Photography'. *Technology and Culture* 15, 1–19.

Jones, K. and Williamson, K. (1979) 'The Birth of the Schoolroom'. *I&C* 6, 59–110.

Kendall, G. (1991) 'Reading the Child Reading: Literacy and the Formation of Citizens in England 1750–1850'. *History of Education Review* 20(2), 79–87.

Kendall, G. and Wickham, G. (1996) 'Governing the Culture of Cities: A Foucaultian Framework'. *Southern Review* 29(2), 202–19.

Knorr-Cetina, K.D. (1981) *The Manufacture of Knowledge*. Oxford: Pergamon.

Kremer-Marietti, A. (1985) *Michel Foucault: Archéologie et généalogie*. Paris: Libraire Générale Française.

Kuhn, T.S. (1970) *The Structure of Scientific Revolutions*. 2nd edn. Chicago: University of Chicago Press.

Laclau, E. and Mouffe, C. (1985) *Hegemony and Socialist Strategy: Towards a Radical Democratic Politics*. London: Verso.

Lakatos, I. and Musgrave, A. (1970) *Criticism and the Growth of Knowledge*. Cambridge: Cambridge University Press.

Language Policy and Guidelines (n.d.) Manchester: Privately printed.

Latour, B. (1987) *Science in Action: How to Follow Engineers in Society*. Milton Keynes: Open University Press.

Latour, B. (1988) *The Pasteurization of France*. Cambridge, Mass.: Harvard University Press.

Latour, B. (1992) 'Where are the Missing Masses?' In Bijker, W. and Law, J. (eds) *Shaping Technology/Building Society*. Cambridge, Mass.: MIT Press.

Latour, B. (1993) *We Have Never Been Modern*. Hemel Hempstead: Harvester Wheatsheaf.

Latour, B. and Woolgar, S. (1986) *Laboratory Life: The Construction of Scientific Facts*. 2nd edn. Princeton: Princeton University Press.

Law, J. (1994) *Organizing Modernity*. Oxford: Blackwell.

Leonard, J. (1980) 'L'historien et le philosophe: à propos de *Surveiller et punir: naissance de la prison*'. In Perrot, M. (ed.) *L'Impossible prison: recherches sur le systeme penitentiaire au XIXe siècle*. Paris: Seuil.

Lewenstein, B.V. (1995) 'Science and the Media'. In Jasanoff, S., Markle, G.E., Peterson, J.C. and Pinch, T. (eds) *Handbook of Science and Technology Studies*. London: Sage.

Lynch, M. (1993) *Scientific Practice and Ordinary Action: Ethnomethodology and Social Studies of Science*. Cambridge: Cambridge University Press.

Mackenzie, D. and Wajcman, J. (eds) (1985) *The Social Shaping of Technology*. Milton Keynes: Open University Press.

Malpas, J. and Wickham, G. (1995) 'Governance and Failure: On the Limits of Sociology'. *Australian and New Zealand Journal of Sociology* 31(3), 37–50.

Malpas, J. and Wickham, G. (1997) 'Governance and the World: From Joe DiMaggio to Michel Foucault'. *The UTS Review* 3(2), 91–108.

Mannheim, K. (1936) *Ideology and Utopia*. New York: Harcourt, Brace and World.

Mannheim, K. (1952) *Essays on the Sociology of Knowledge*. London: Routledge and Kegan Paul.

Marx, K. (1973) *Grundrisse*. Harmondsworth: Penguin.

Marx, K. and Engels, F. (1965) *Manifesto of the Communist Party*. Moscow: Progress Press.

Megill, A. (1985) *Prophets of Extremity: Nietzsche, Heidegger, Foucault, Derrida*. Berkeley: University of California Press.

Merton, R.K. (1970) *Science, Technology and Society in Seventeenth-Century England*. New York: Harper and Row.

Merton, R.K. (1973) *The Sociology of Science*. Chicago: University of Chicago Press.

Miller, P. and O'Leary, T. (1994) 'The Factory as Laboratory'. *Science in Context* 7(3), 469–96.

Miller, P. and Rose, N. (1990) 'Governing Economic Life'. *Economy and Society* 19(1), 1–31.

Miller, T. (1993) *The Well-Tempered Self: Citizenship, Culture, and the Postmodern Subject*. Baltimore: Johns Hopkins University Press.

Mulkay, M.J. (1979) *Science and the Sociology of Knowledge*. London: Allen and Unwin.

Nelkin, D. (1987) *Selling Science*. New York: Freeman.

Pearson, H. (1985) *Children Becoming Readers*. London: Macmillan.

Peters, E. (1985) *Torture*. Oxford: Blackwell.

Piaget, J. (1959) *The Language and Thought of the Child*. London: Routledge and Kegan Paul.

Popper, K. (1959) *The Logic of Scientific Discovery*. New York: Harper and Row.

Popper, K. (1963) *Conjectures and Refutations: The Growth of Scientific Knowledge*. London: Routledge and Kegan Paul.

Raban, B. and Moon, C. (1978) *Books and Learning to Read*. Oxford: School Library Association.

Rabinow, P. (1989) *French Modern: Norms and Forms of the Social Environment*. Cambridge, Mass.: MIT Press.

Ritzer, G. (1992) *Sociological Theory*. 3rd edn. New York: McGraw-Hill.

Rose, N. (1984) 'The Formation of the Psychology of the Individual in England 1870–1939'. Unpublished PhD thesis, University of London.

Rose, N. (1985) *The Psychological Complex: Psychology, Politics and Society in England 1869–1939*. London: Routledge and Kegan Paul.

Rose, N. (1990) 'Of Madness Itself: *Histoire de la Folie* and the Object of Psychiatric History'. *History of the Human Sciences* 3(3), 373–80.

Rose, N. (1991) 'Governing by Numbers: Figuring Out Democracy'. *Accounting, Organization and Society* 16(7), 673–92.

Rose, N. (1992a) 'Towards a Critical Sociology of Freedom'. Inaugural lecture, Goldsmiths College, University of London.

Rose, N. (1992b) *Governing the Soul*. London: Routledge.

Sawicki, J. (1991) *Disciplining Foucault: Feminism, Power, and the Body*. London: Routledge.

Schaffer, S. (1992) 'Self-Evidence'. *Critical Inquiry* 18, 327–62.

Schwarz, M. and Thompson, M. (1990) *Divided We Stand: Redefining Politics, Technology and Social Choice*. Hemel Hempstead: Harvester Wheatsheaf.

Sextus Empiricus (1994) *Outlines of Scepticism*. Cambridge: Cambridge University Press.

Shapin, S. (1988) 'The House of Experiment in Seventeenth-Century England'. *Isis* 79, 373–404.

Shapin, S. and Schaffer, S. (1985) *Leviathan and the Air-Pump: Hobbes, Boyle, and the Experimental Life*. Princeton: Princeton University Press.

Silverman, D. (ed.) (1997) *Qualitative Research: Theory, Method and Practice*. London: Sage.

Star, S.L. and Griesemer, J.R. (1989) 'Institutional Ecology, "Translations" and Boundary Objects: Amateurs and Professionals in Berkeley's Museum of Vertebrate Zoology, 1907–39'. *Social Studies of Science* 19, 387–420.

Stark, W. (1958) *The Sociology of Knowledge*. London: Routledge and Kegan Paul.

Stow, D. (1836) *The Training System Adopted in the Model Schools of the Glasgow Educational Society; a Manual for Infant and Juvenile Schools, which Includes a System of Moral Training Suited to the Condition of Large Towns*. Glasgow: W.R. McPhun.

Stow, D. (1839) *National Education. Supplement to Moral Education and the Training System, with Plans for Erecting and Fitting Up Training Schools*. Glasgow: W.R. McPhun.

Stow, D. (1850) *The Training System, the Moral Training School, and the Normal Seminary*. London: Longman, Brown, Green.

Szilard, L. (1978) *Leo Szilard: His Version of the Facts*. Cambridge, Mass.: MIT Press.

Taylor, C. (1985) 'Foucault on Freedom and Truth'. In *Philosophy and the Human Sciences: Philosophical Papers II*. Cambridge: Cambridge University Press.

Tyler, D. (1993) 'Making Better Children'. In Meredyth, D. and Tyler, D. (eds) *Child and Citizen: Genealogies of Schooling and Subjectivity*. Brisbane: Institute for Cultural Policy Studies, Griffith University.

Venn, C. (1984) 'The Subject of Psychology'. In Henriques, J., Hollway, W., Urwin, C., Venn, C. and Walkerdine, V. *Changing the Subject: Psychology, Social Regulation and Subjectivity*. London: Methuen.

Walkerdine, V. (1984) 'Developmental Psychology and the Child-Centred Pedagogy: The Insertion of Piaget into Early Education'. In Henriques, J., Hollway, W., Urwin, C., Venn, C. and Walkerdine, V. *Changing the Subject: Psychology, Social Regulation and Subjectivity*. London: Methuen.

Walkerdine, V. (1988) *The Mastery of Reason*. London: Routledge.

Weber, M. (1989) *The Protestant Ethic and the Spirit of Capitalism*. London: Unwin Hyman.

White, L. (1962) *Medieval Technology and Social Change*. London: Open University Press.

Williams, B. (1993) *Shame and Necessity*. Berkeley: University of California Press.

Willis, P.E. (1977) *Learning to Labour: How Working Class Kids Get Working Class Jobs*. Aldershot: Ashgate.

Woolgar, S. (1988) *Science: The Very Idea*. London: Tavistock.

Yamamoto, T. (1997) 'Director's Note'. *iichiko intercultural: An Annual Journal for Transdisciplinary Studies of Pratiques* 9, 3–5.

Index